Jonathan Mumaw AKA "Hence Da Meat" is a self-taught multimedia creative artist. Inspired by hip-hop/rap, graffiti, and skateboarding. He found a love for all types of music genres, art, fashion, and a nak for colors while working in the paint department in a home improvement store at an early age. Today, he makes the type of art that he wants to see on his shelf. If you like something "make it." "Hence" this book!

Instagram- @hencedameat

Website- www.hencedameat.com

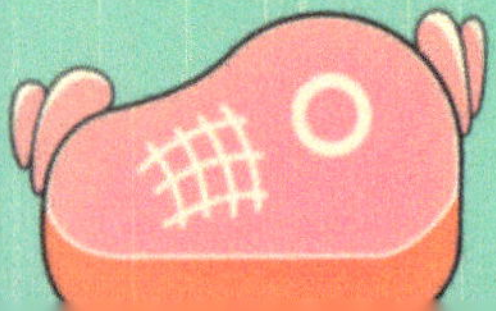

I want to dedicate this book to my wonderful life partner Kimberly Inthavong! She makes me feel like I can conquer the world and that I can accomplish anything! Without her this book wouldn't be possible!

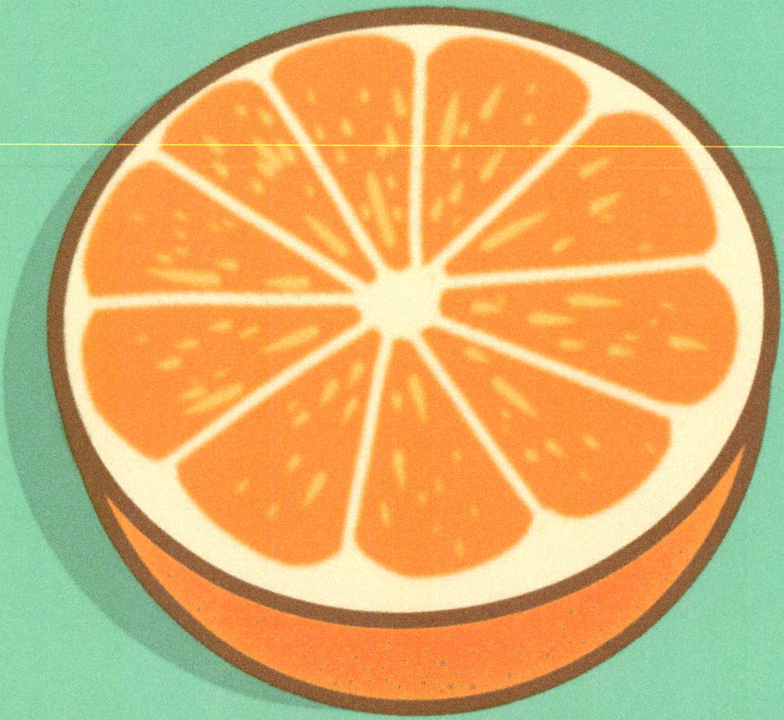

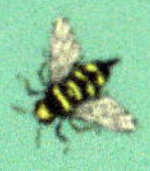

Written by Jonathan Mumaw
Illustrated by "Hence" Da Meat

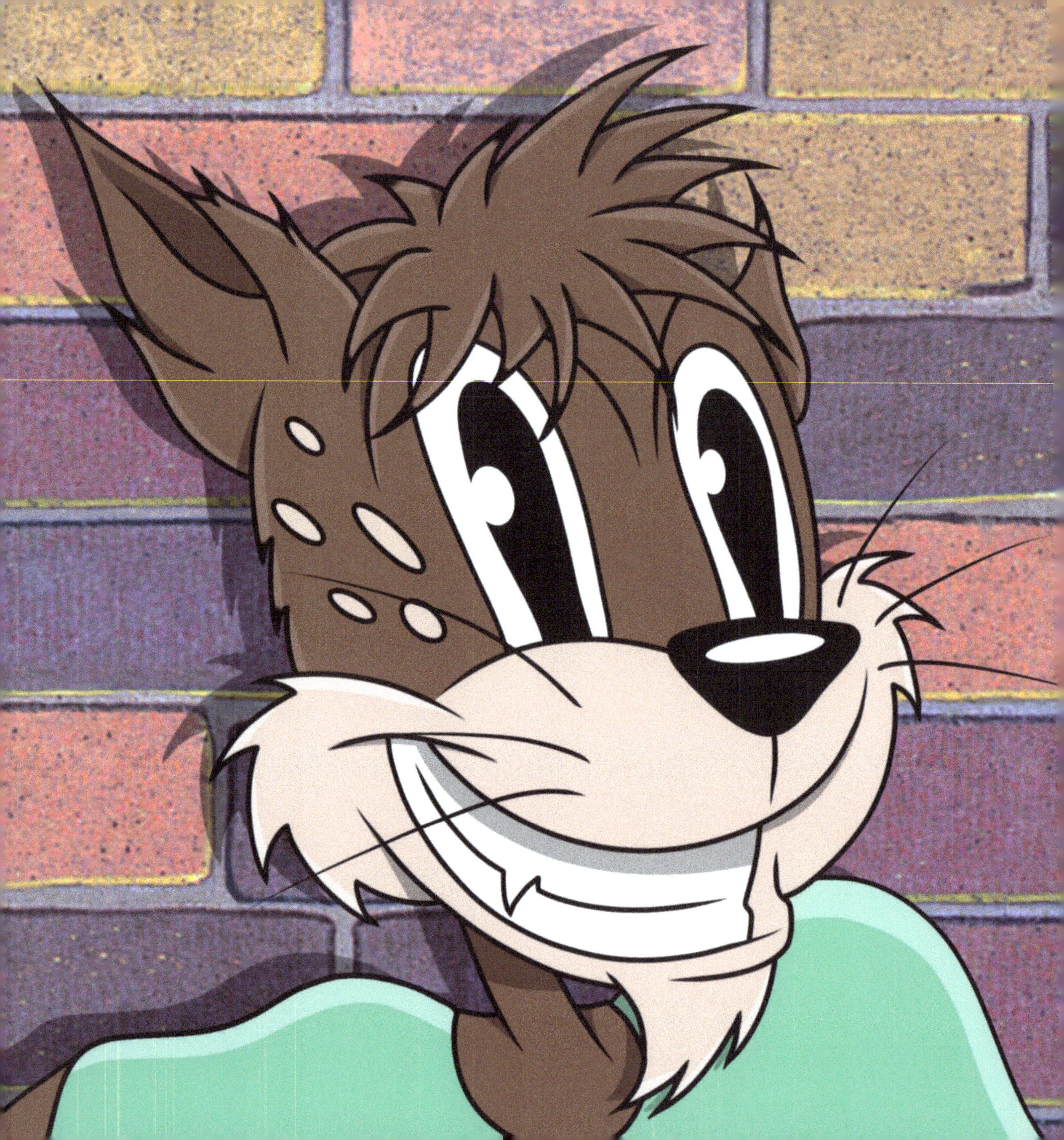

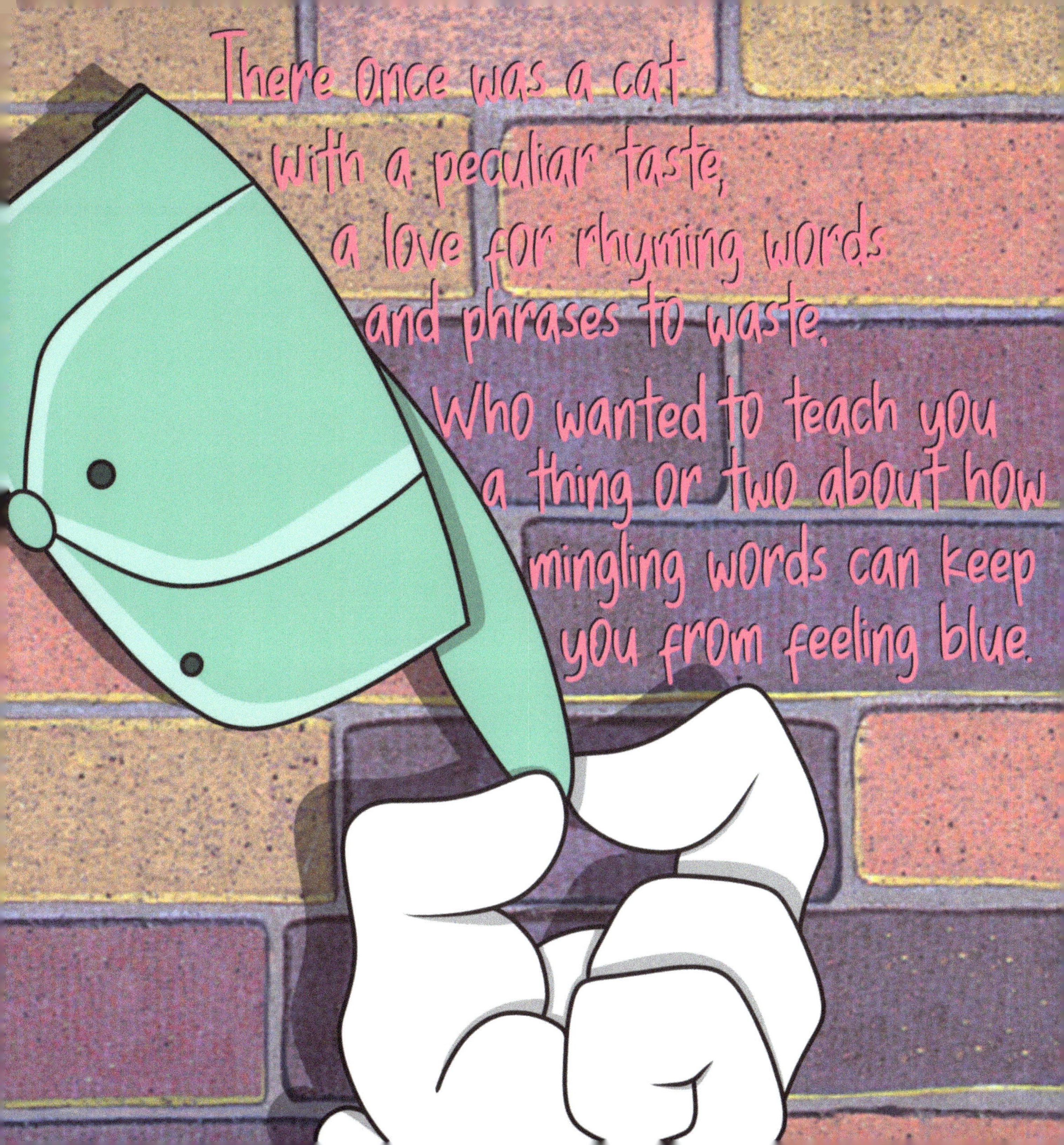

There once was a cat
with a peculiar taste,
a love for rhyming words
and phrases to waste.
Who wanted to teach you
a thing or two about how
mingling words can keep
you from feeling blue.

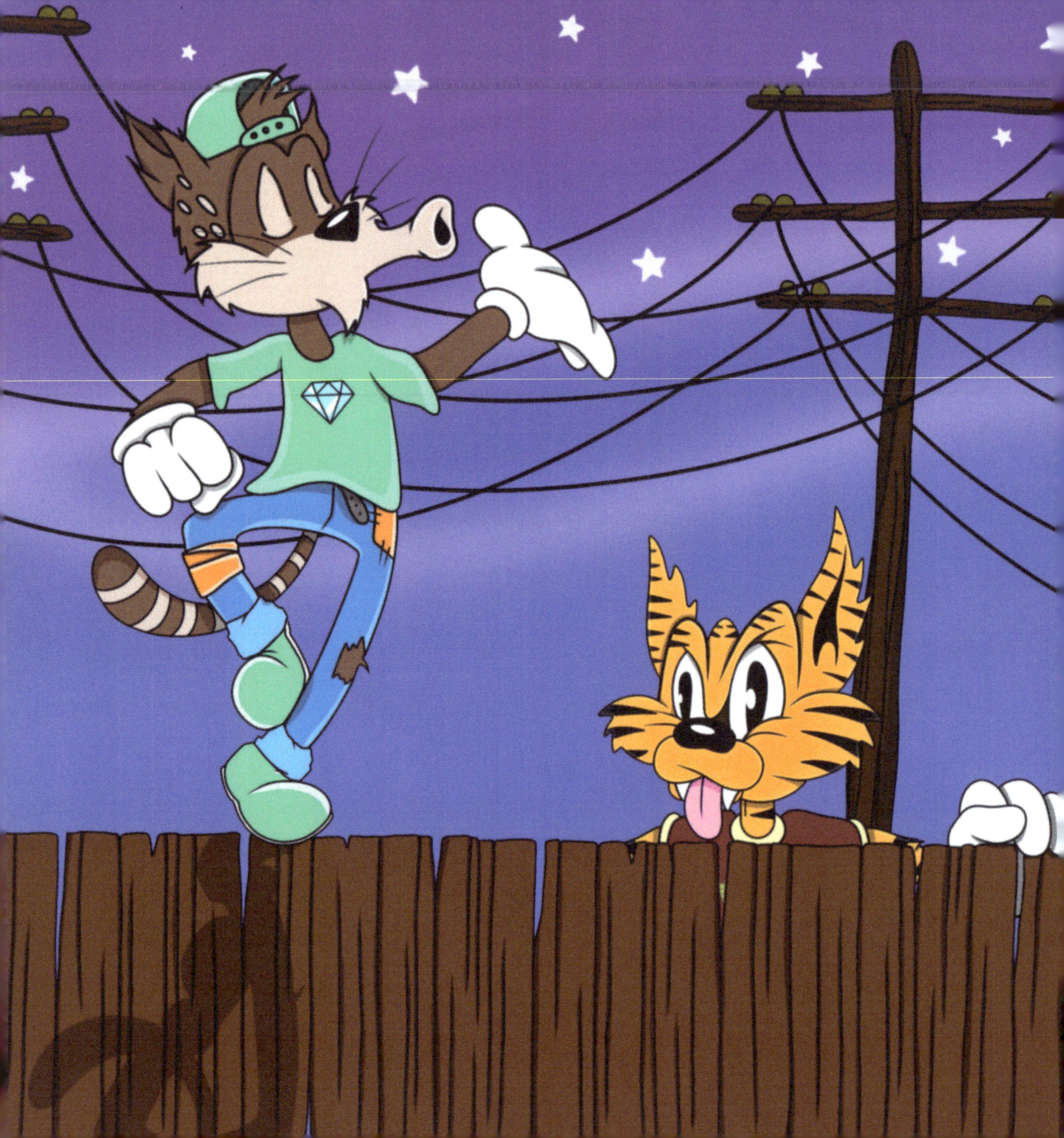

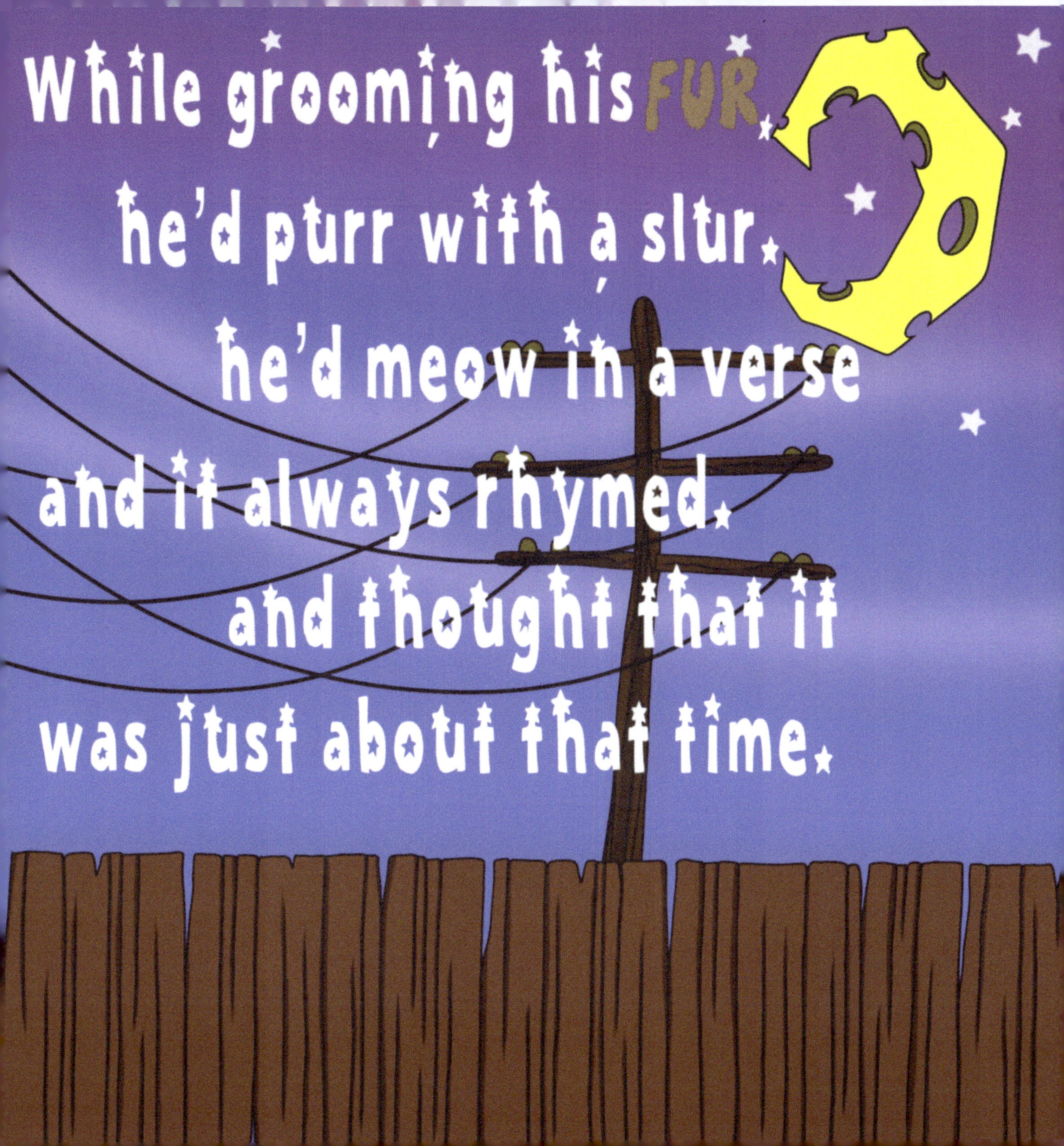

While grooming his FUR,
he'd purr with a slur,
he'd meow in a verse
and it always rhymed,
and thought that it
was just about that time.

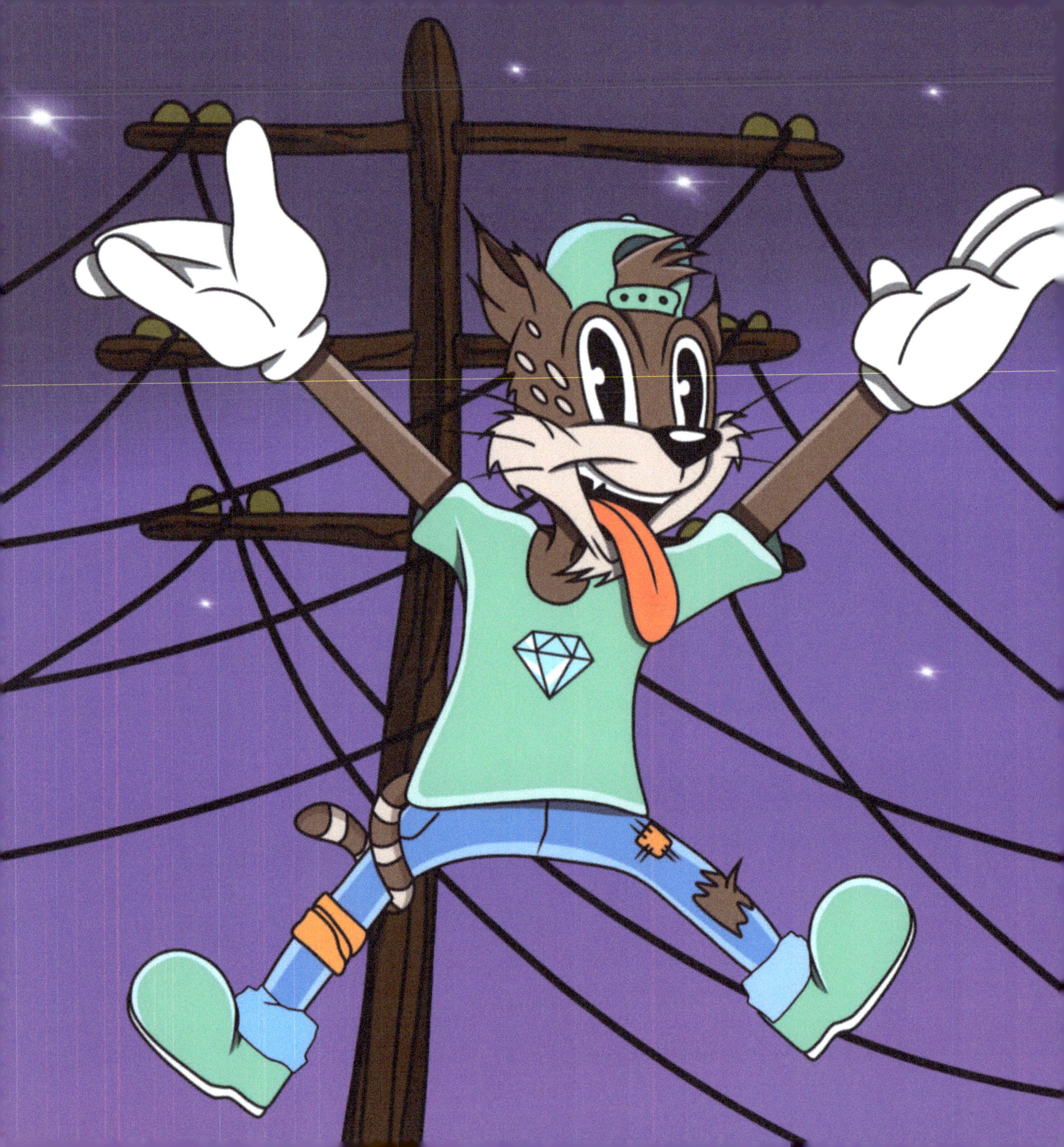

He said, "Just to let you know,

I'm wacky and that's a fact.

Besides that, my name is Jack!

So turn to the next page before
it fades to black!"

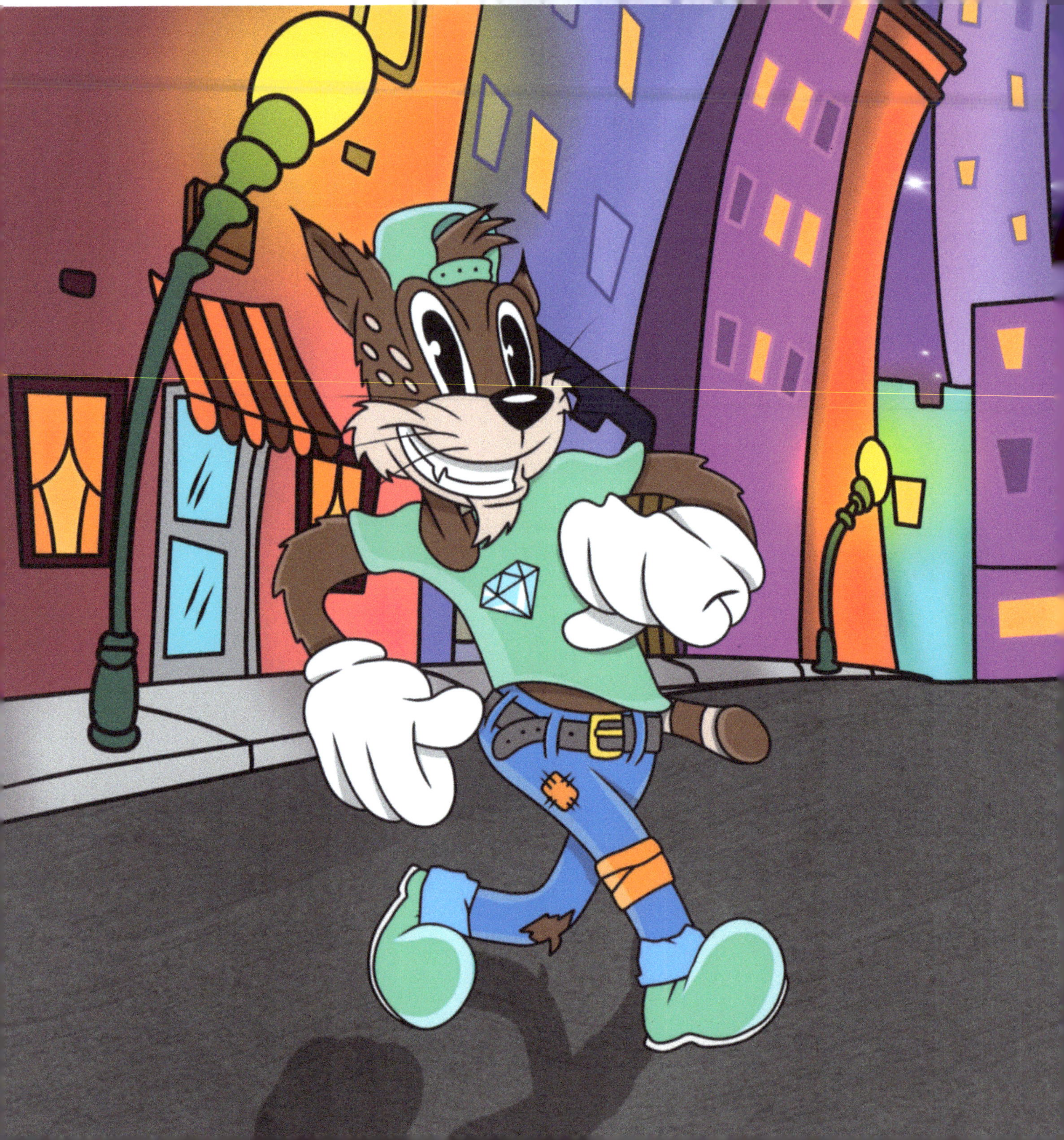

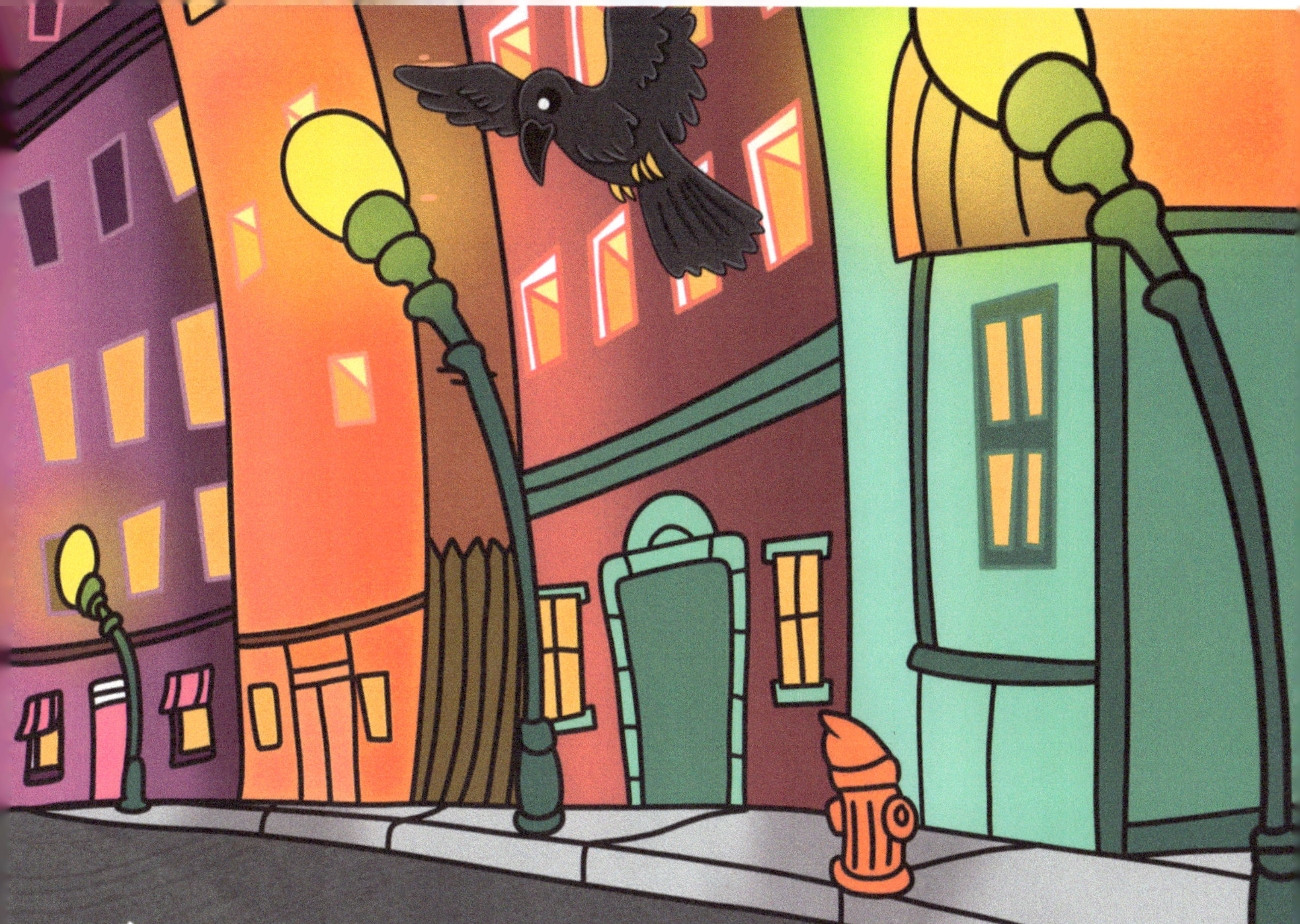

"So come along with me, and you shall see
that rhyming is fun, don't you agree?
While I prowl the streets
saying words that jingle,
I like to learn new words that mingle.

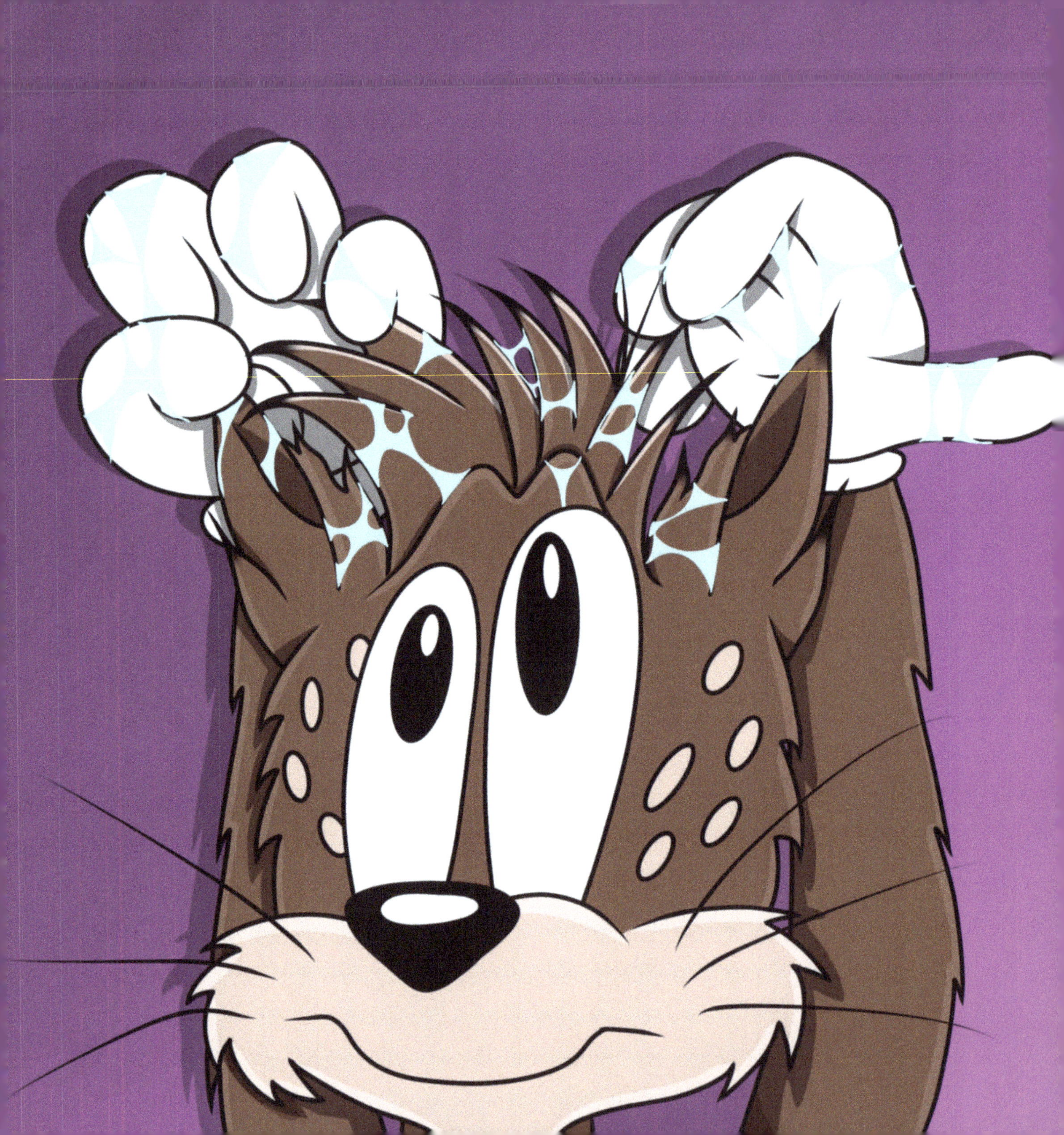

Like that time I
mingled a word like
shampoo
and rhymed it with
a word like
Glue.

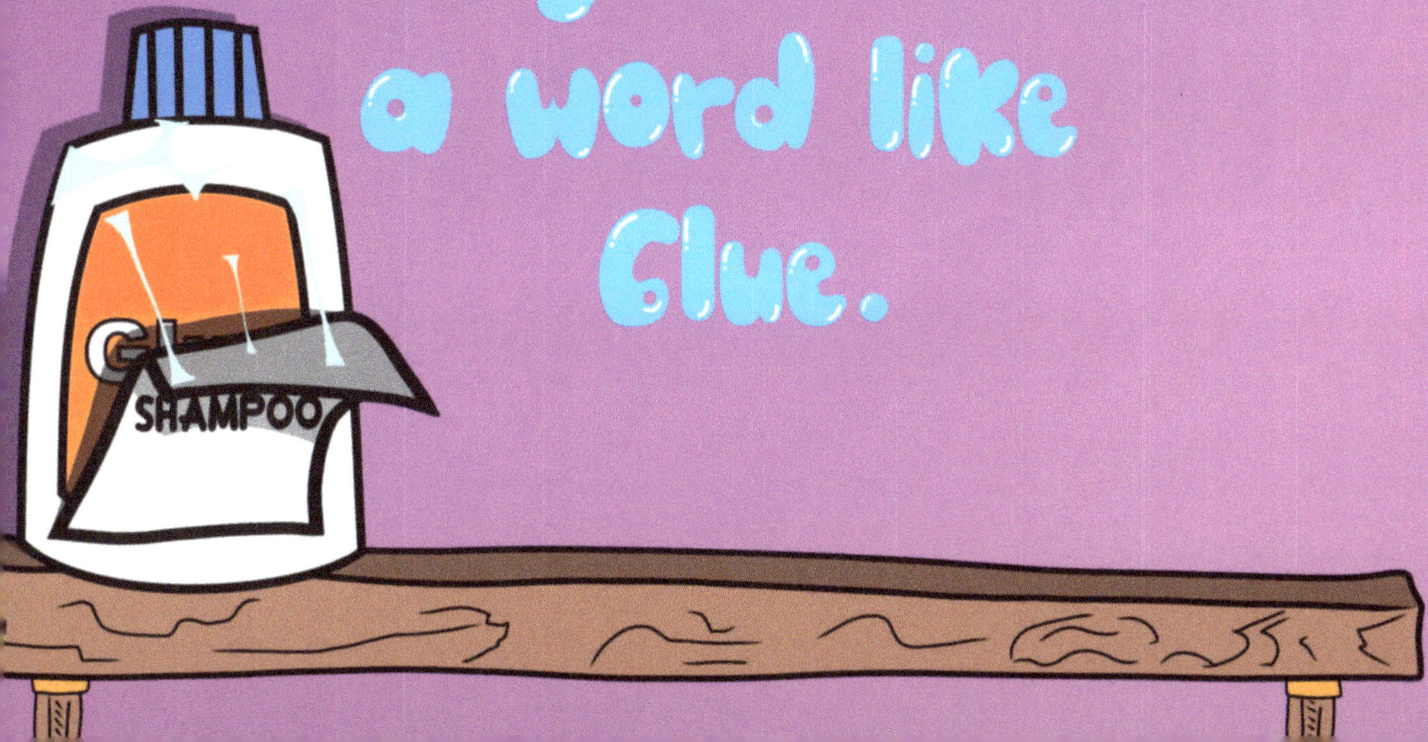

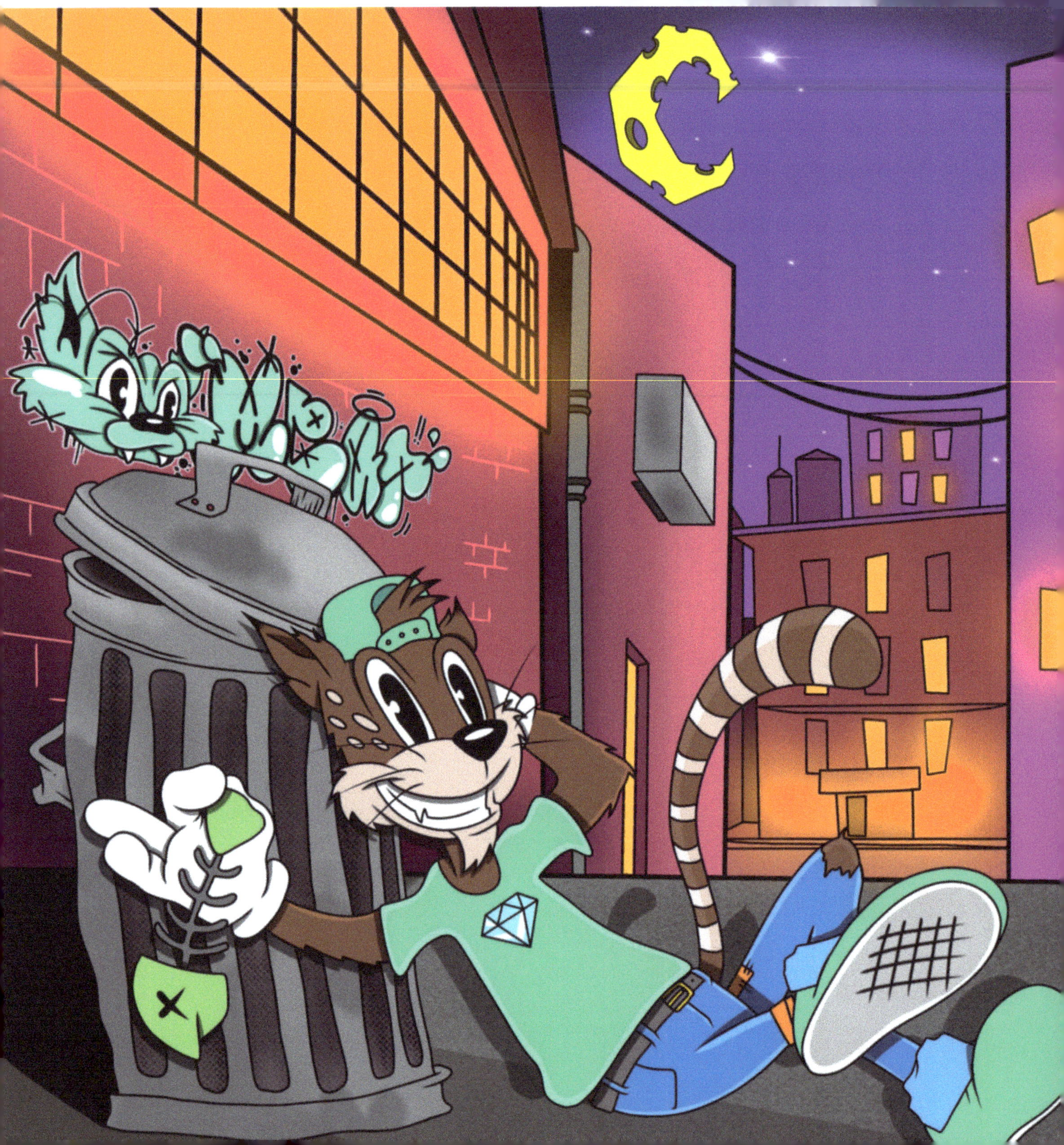

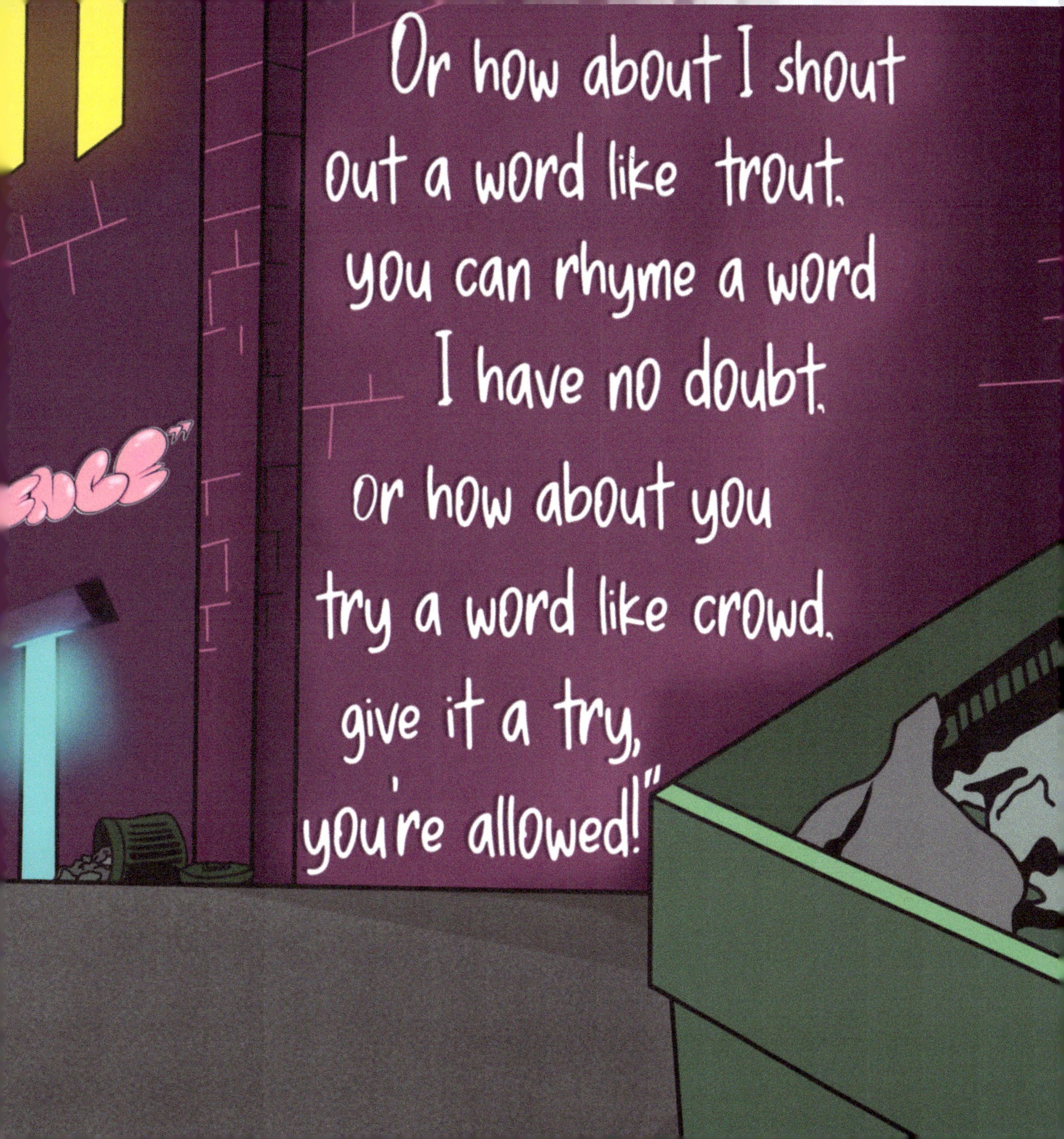

Or how about I shout
out a word like trout,
you can rhyme a word
I have no doubt.
Or how about you
try a word like crowd,
give it a try,
you're allowed!"

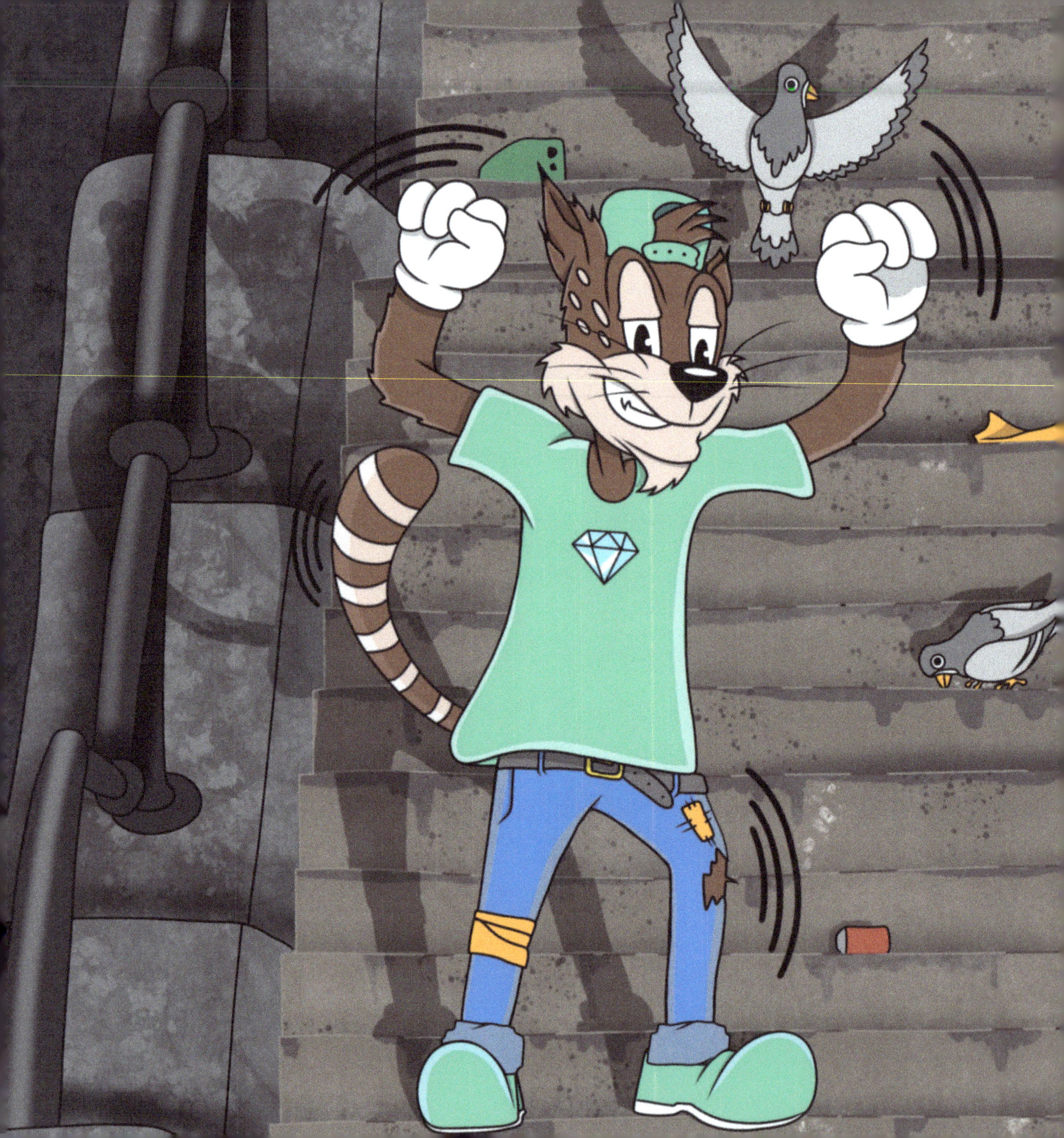

I am a jack of all trades, I am not a joker.
I am unique and not mediocre.
In rhyme, I remind myself that I am great
and on a path that is free from hate,
free from fears, and free from tears,
I will love myself throughout the years.
If I am ever feeling sad,
I remind myself that I am rad.
I rhyme while I dance around,
I laugh so hard I hit the ground.

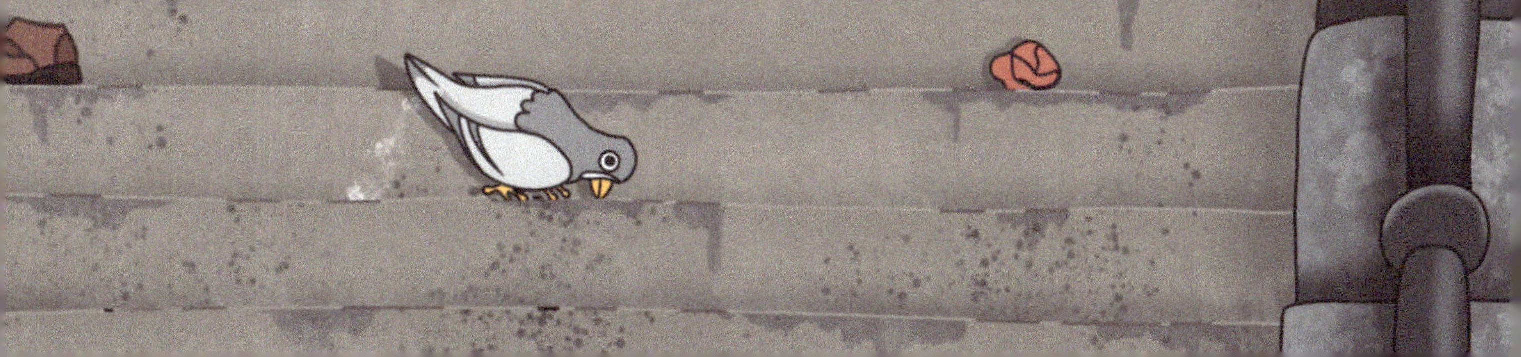

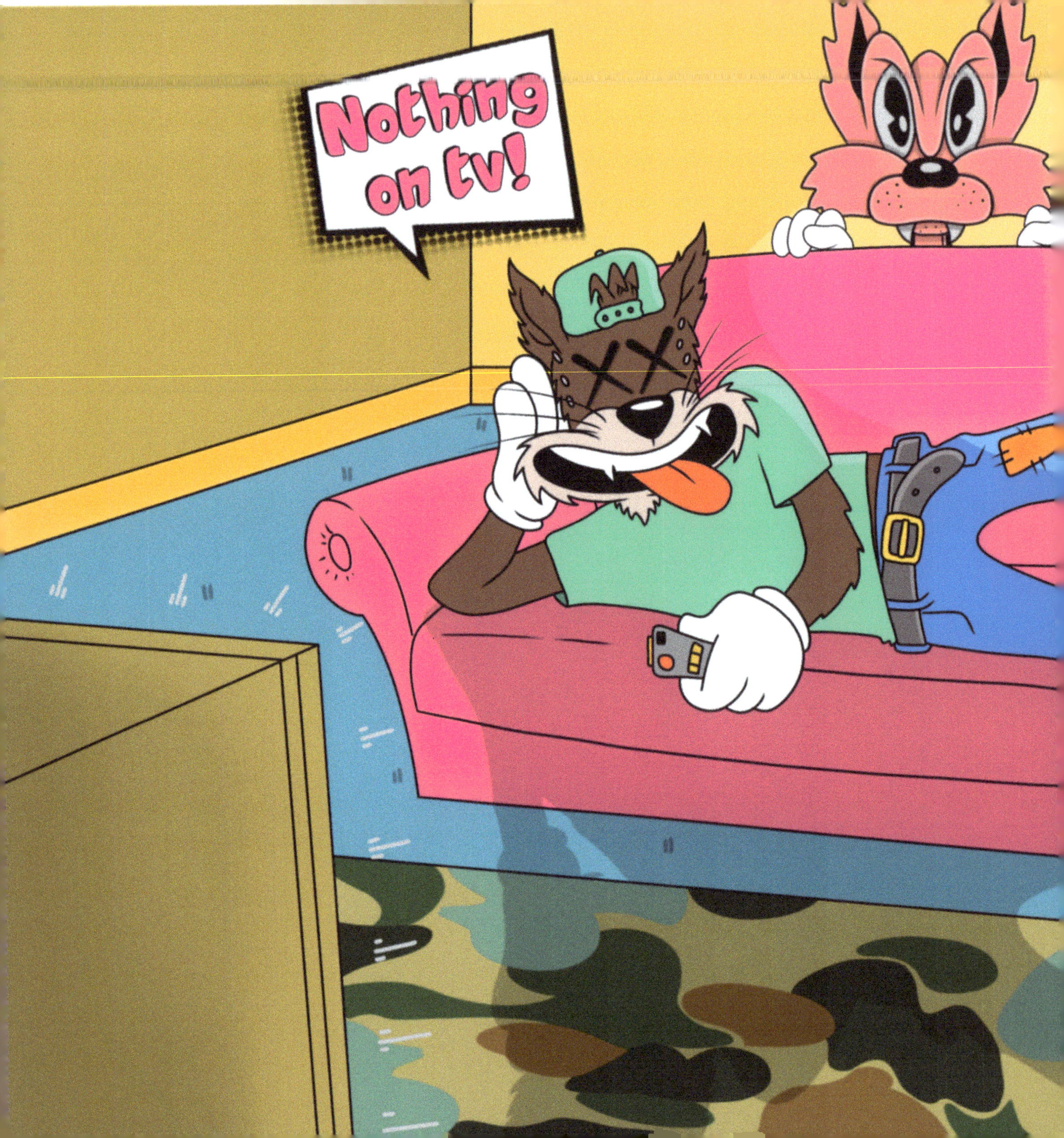
Nothing on tv!

"As the day draws to a close
and I started to tire,
I made my way home,
so that I can retire.

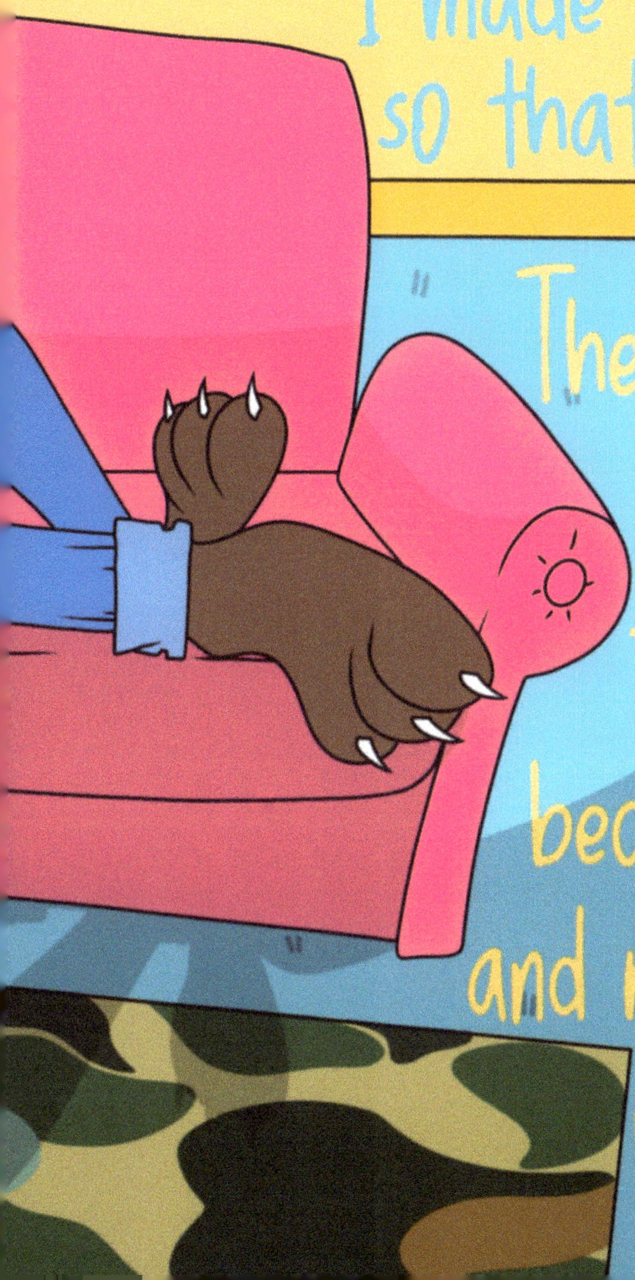

"There's nothing on television,
so I make the decision
to get a good nights rest
because that's what I desire
and refresh my brain so that
my rhymes may be fire."

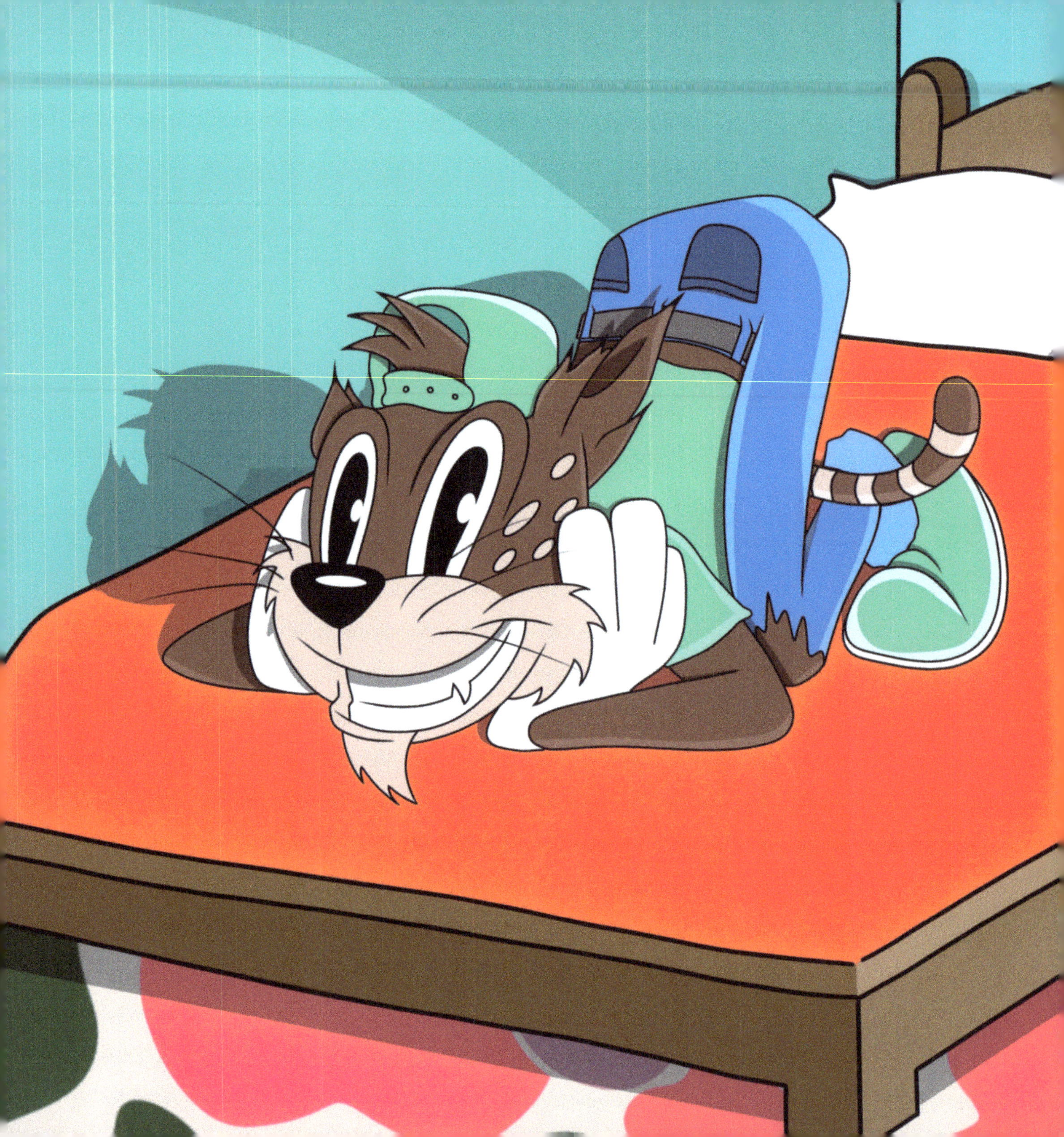

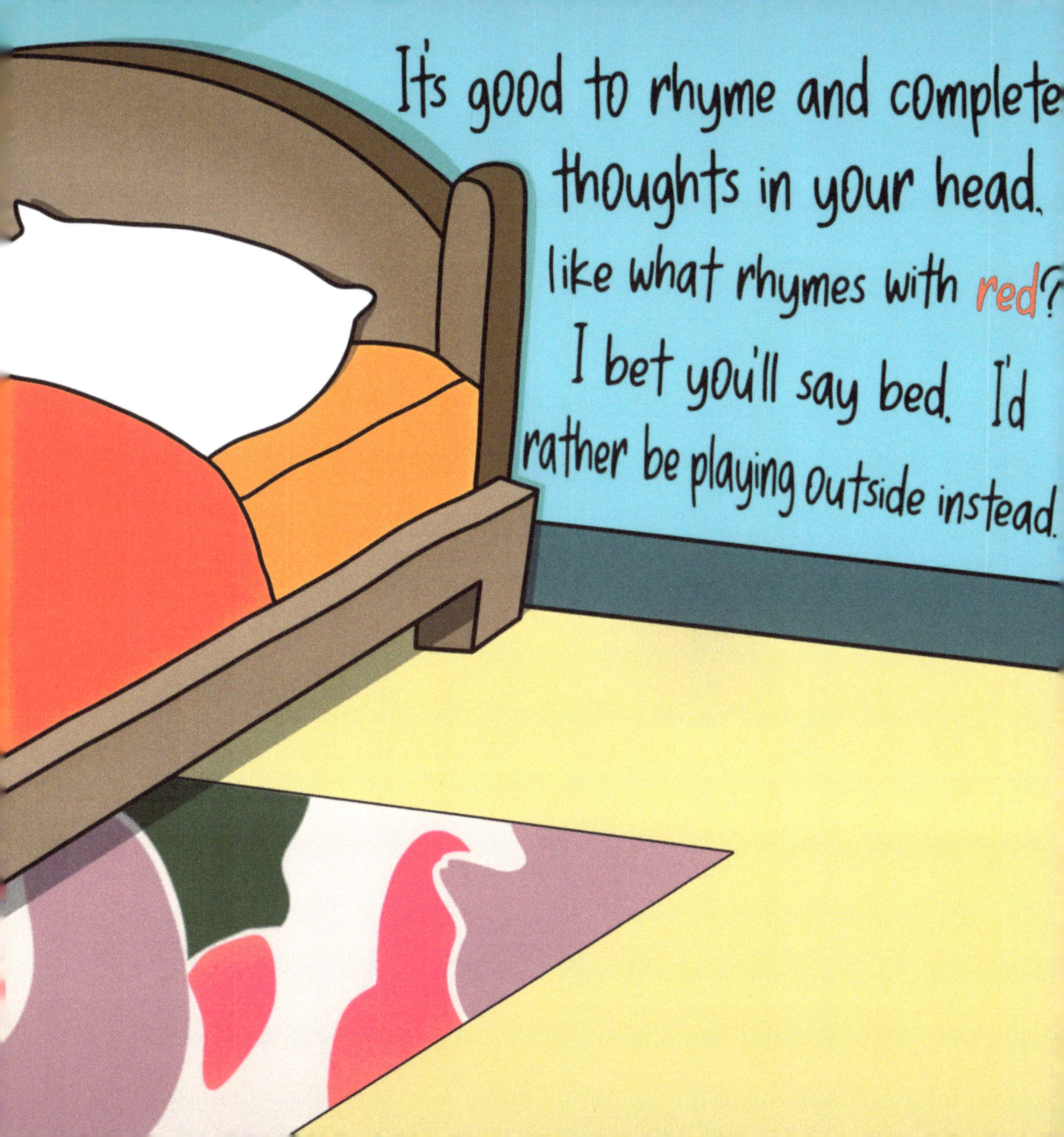

It's good to rhyme and complete thoughts in your head. like what rhymes with red? I bet you'll say bed. I'd rather be playing outside instead.

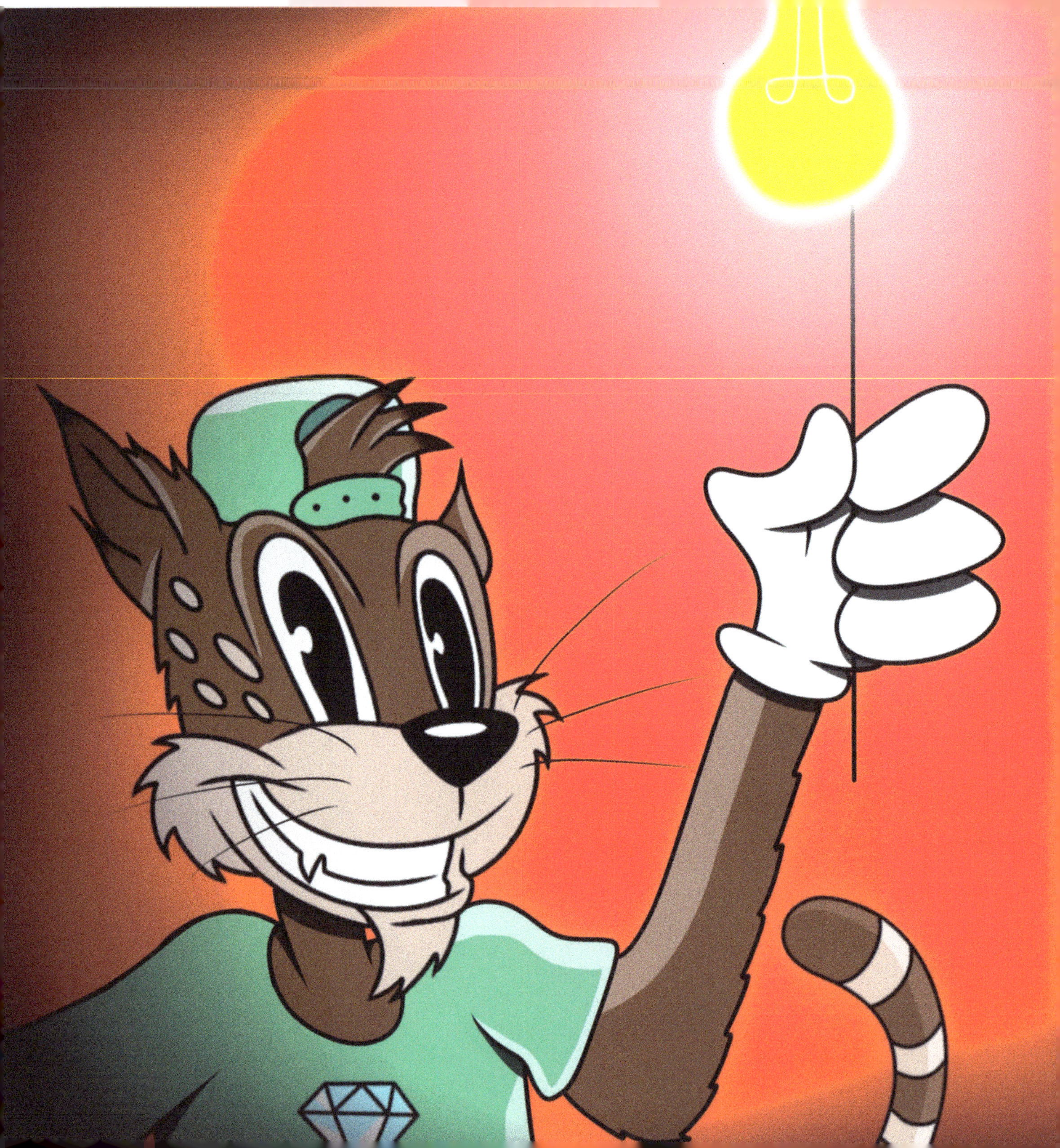

Rhyming is so cool,
it helps you learn
like a magic tool.
In your brain,
it makes a spark,
rhyming words
light up the dark."

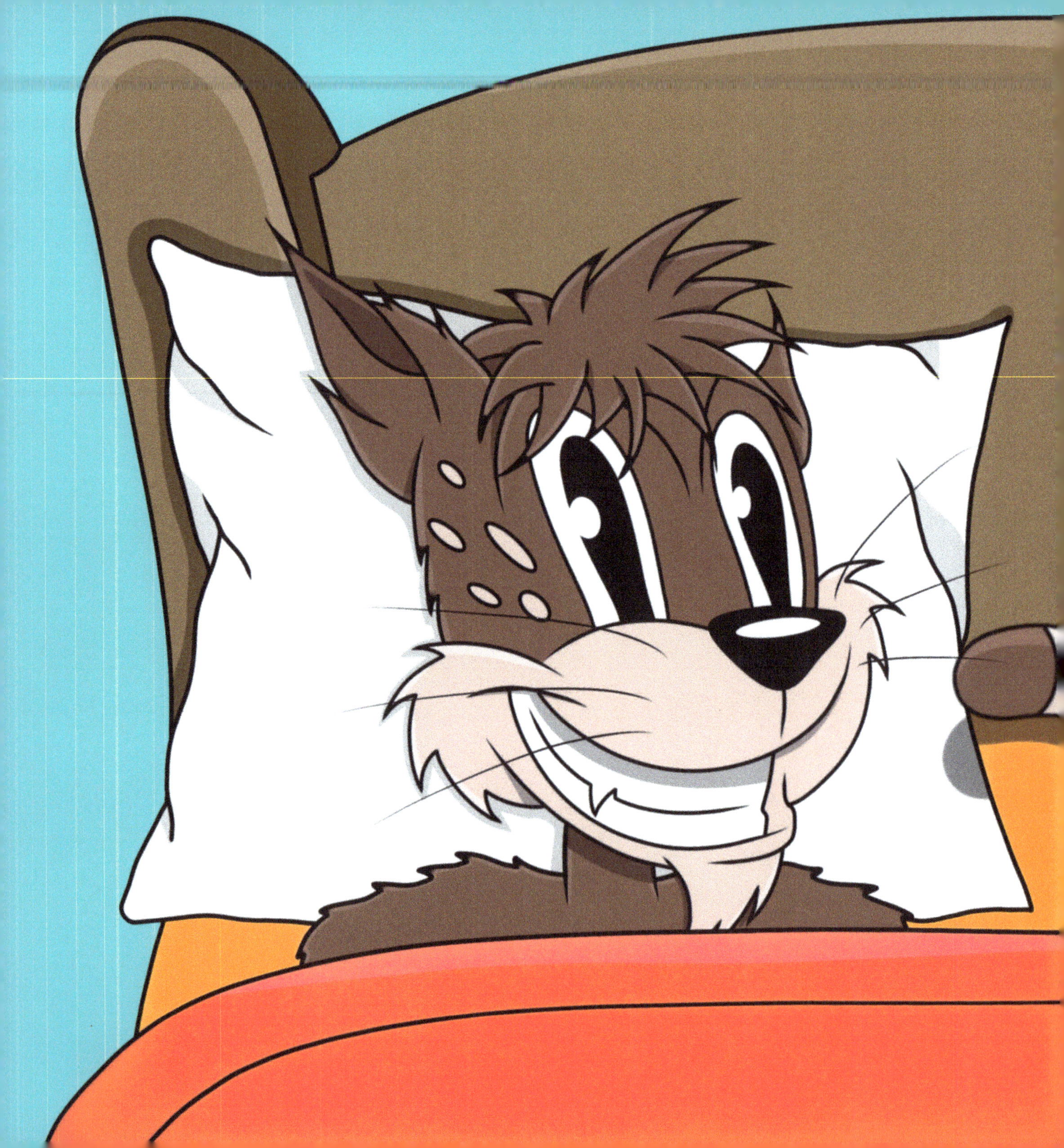

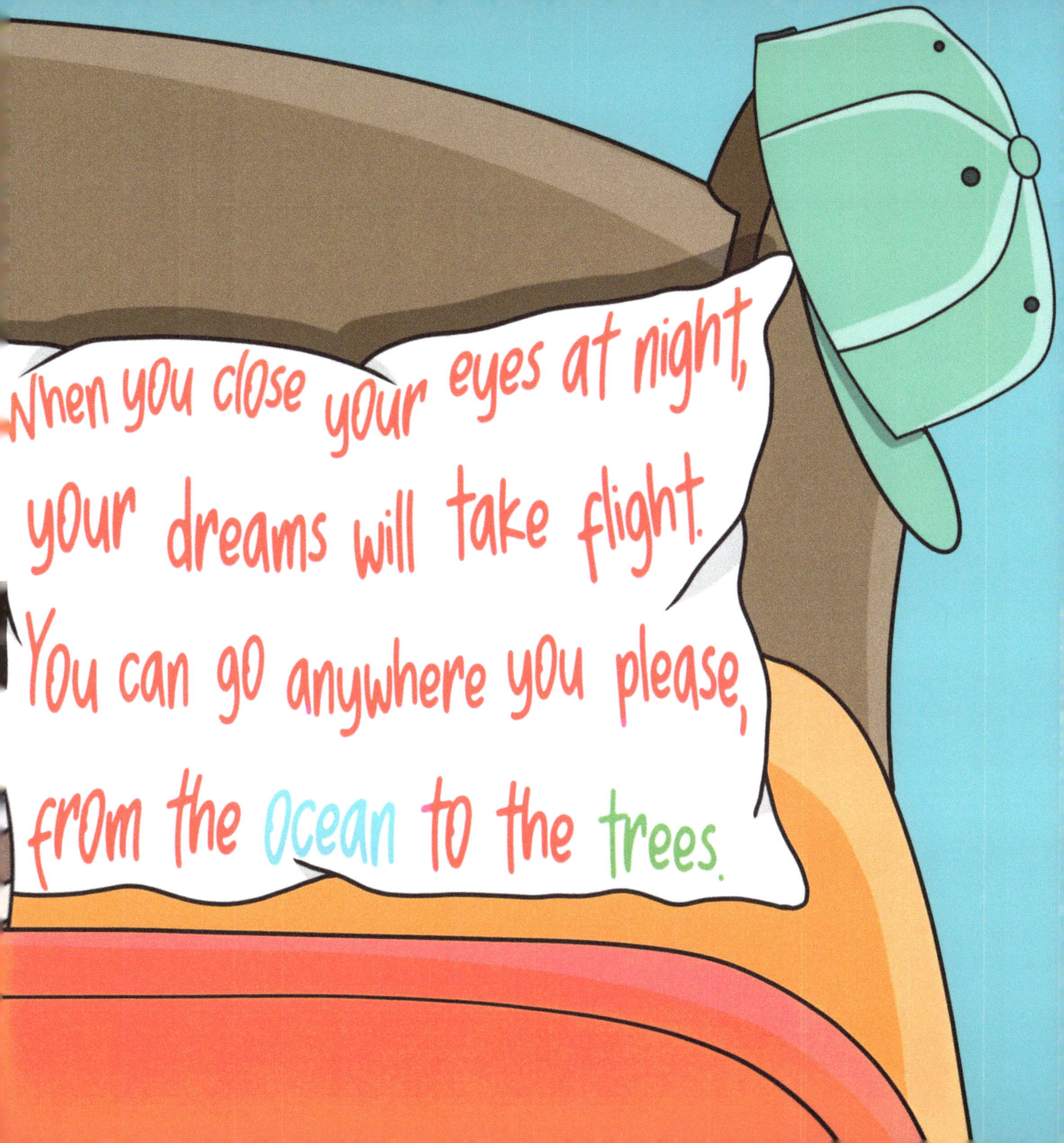

When you close your eyes at night,
your dreams will take flight.
You can go anywhere you please,
from the ocean to the trees.

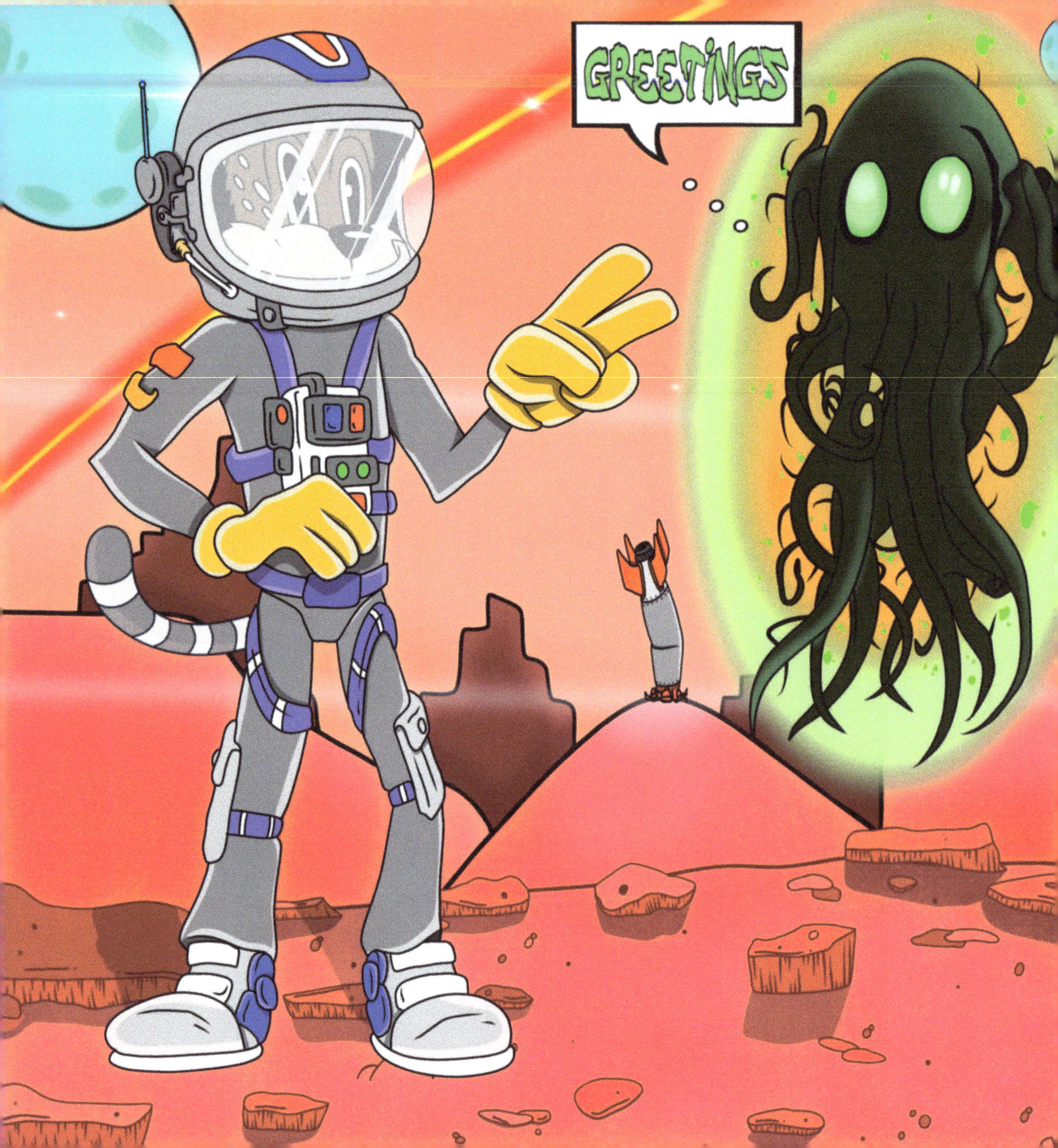
GREETINGS

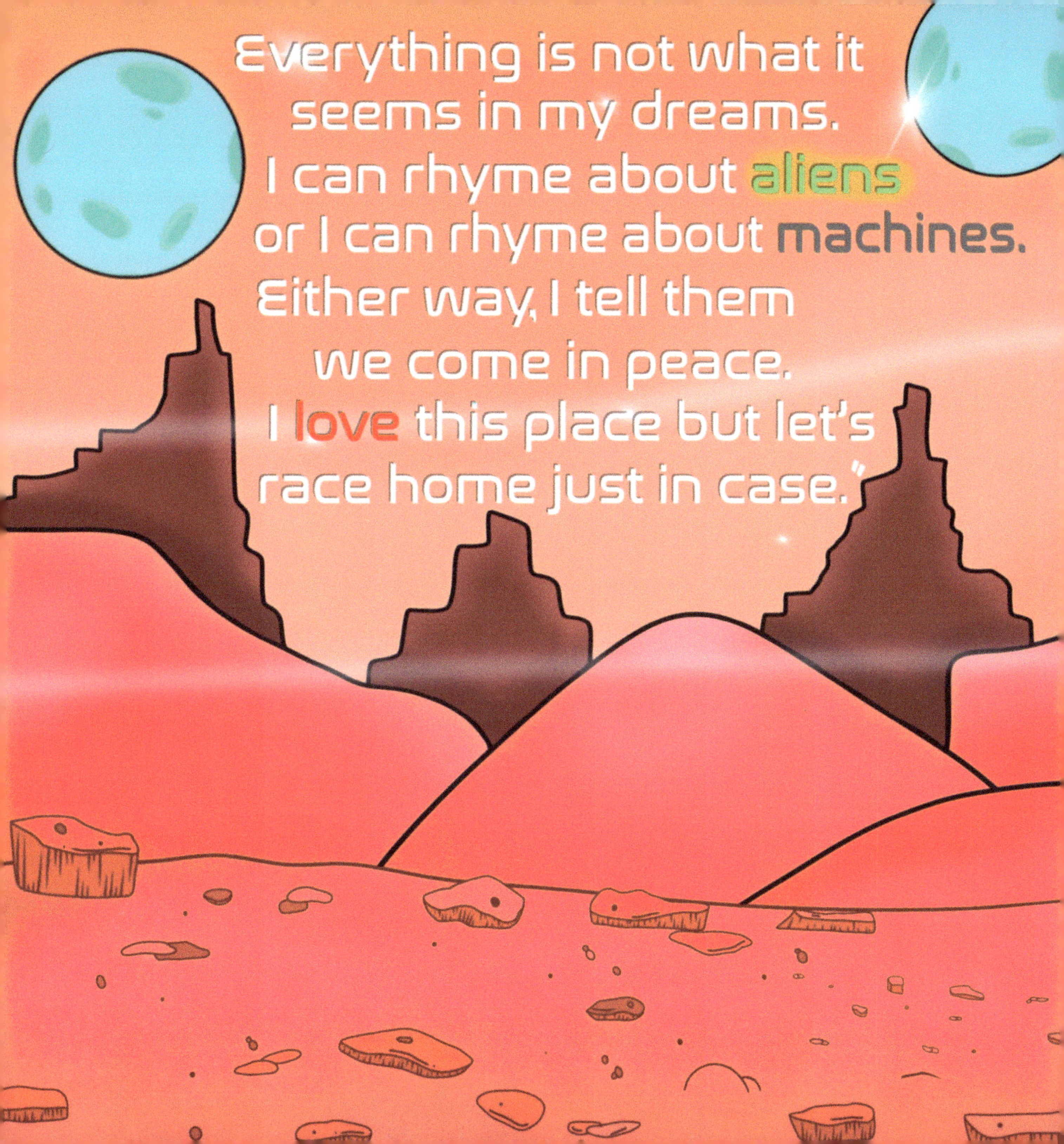

Everything is not what it
seems in my dreams.
I can rhyme about aliens
or I can rhyme about machines.
Either way, I tell them
we come in peace.
I love this place but let's
race home just in case."

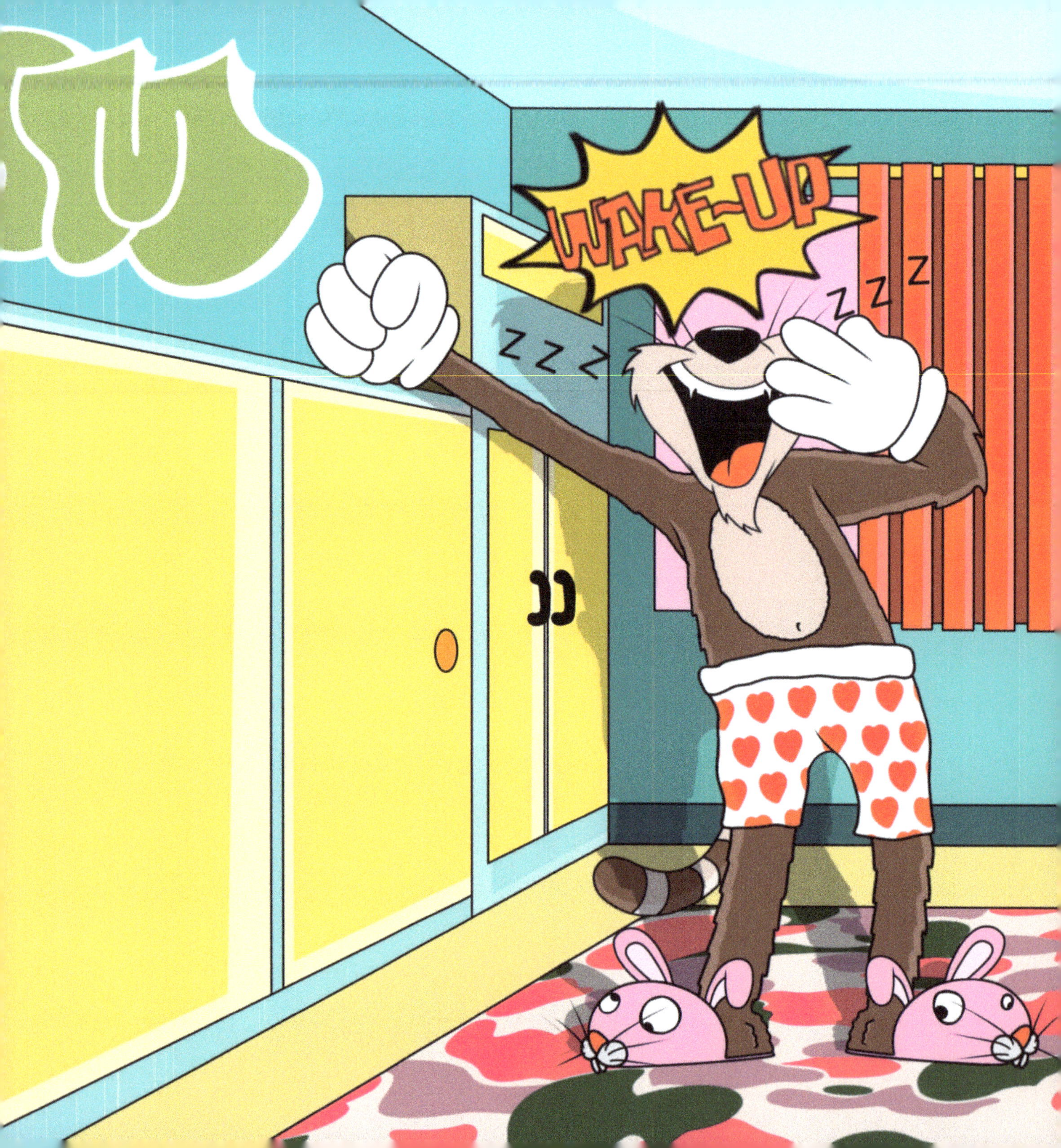
WAKE-UP
ZZZ
ZZZ

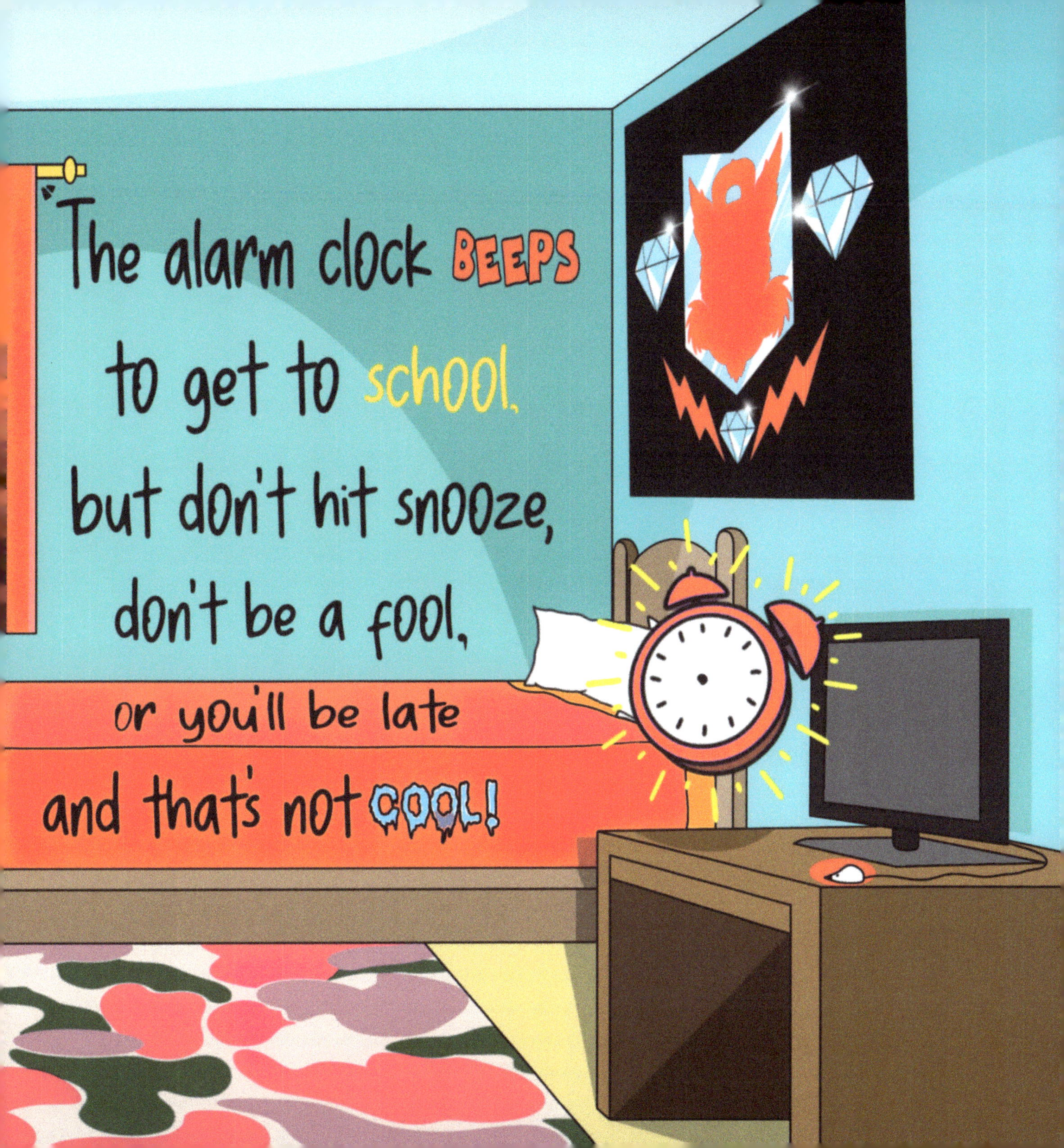

The alarm clock BEEPS
to get to school,
but don't hit snooze,
don't be a fool,
or you'll be late
and that's not COOL!

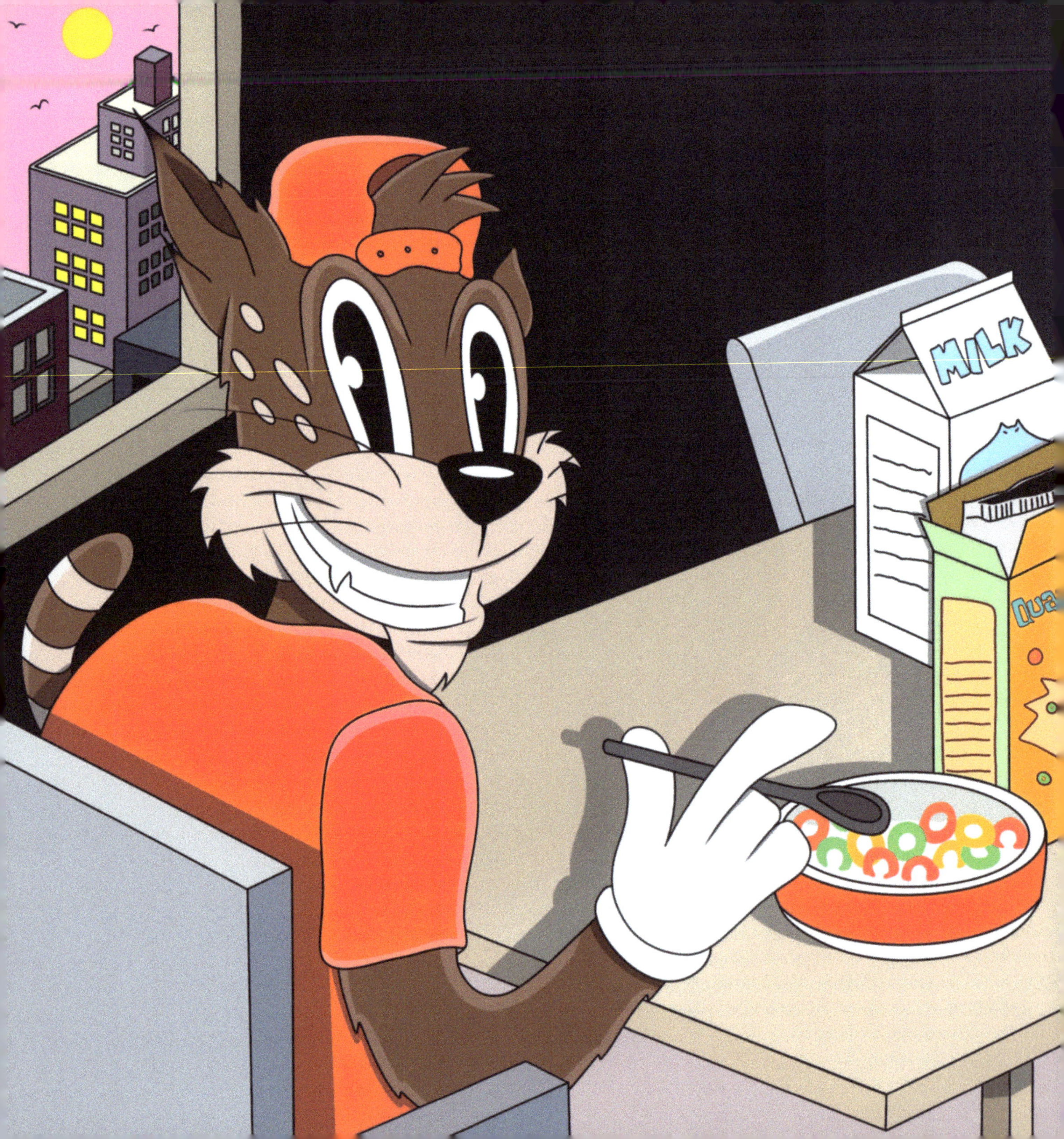
MILK

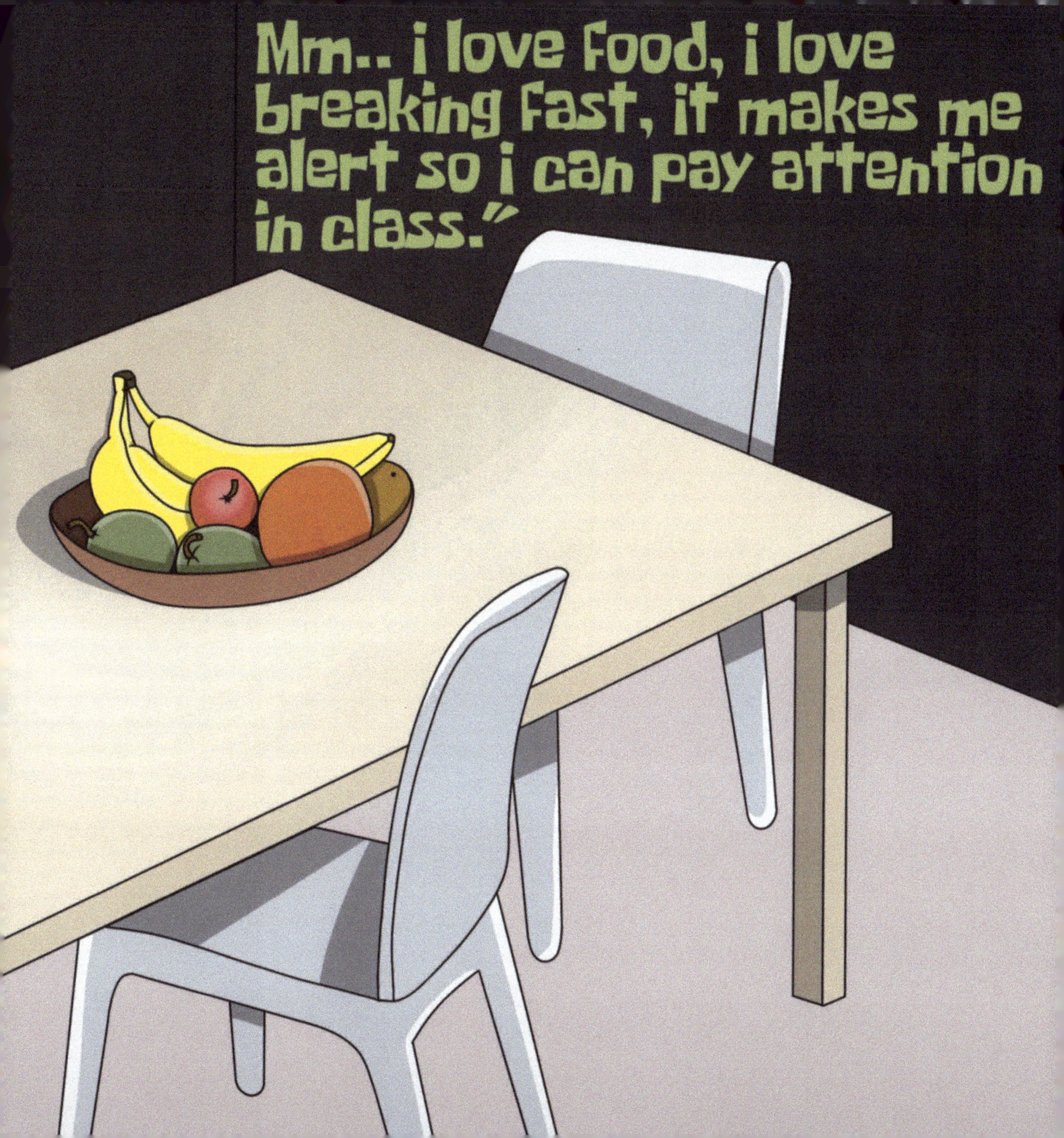
Mm.. i love food, i love breaking fast, it makes me alert so i can pay attention in class."

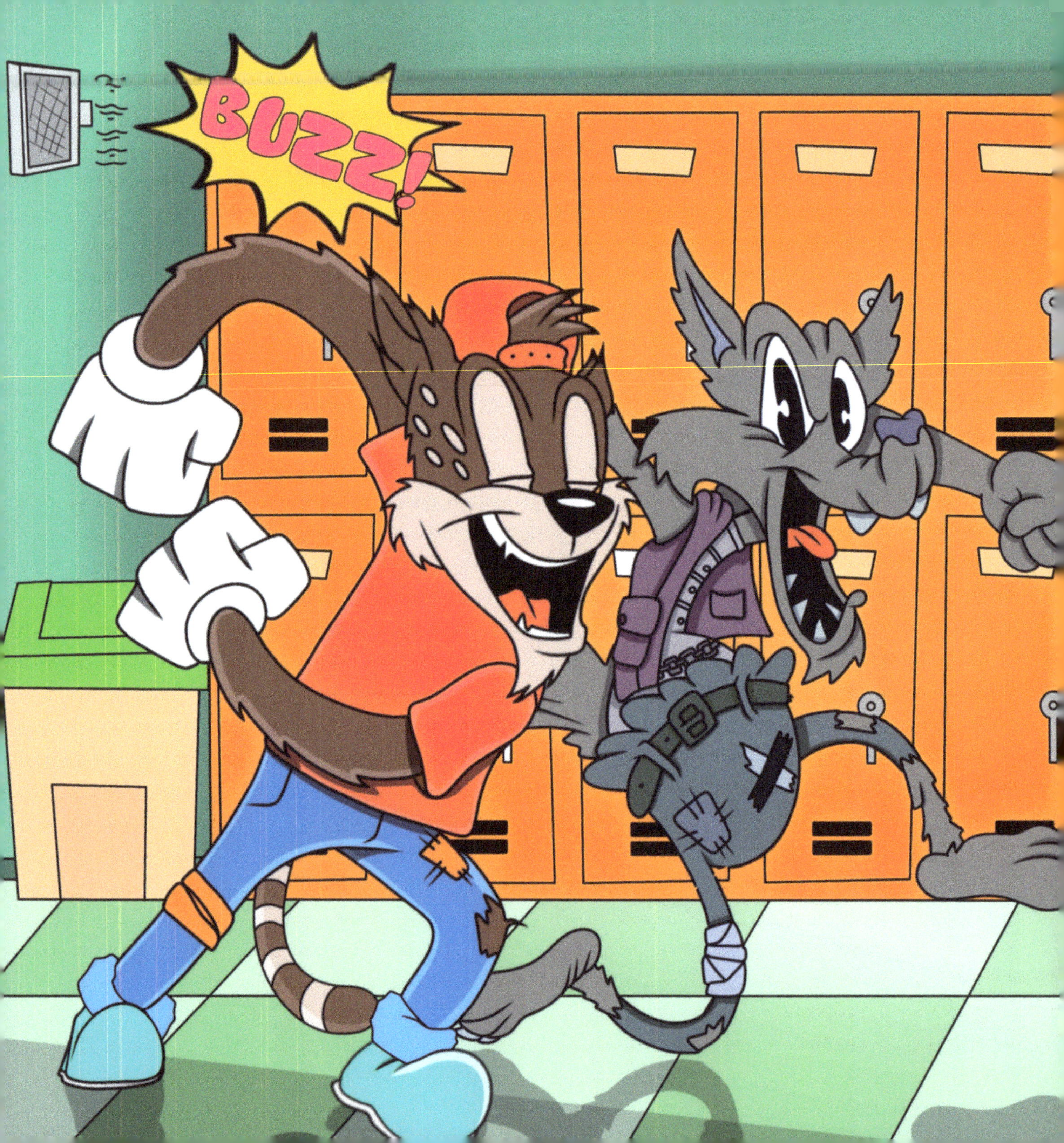
BUZZ!

"As I start another day of school,
being on the ball is the rule.
So we're off to class without delay,
we'll make it just in time, hooray!
Unlocking our lockers with precision,
preparing for another mission.
The janitor's hard work and dedication
ensures a clean and tidy education.
We catch a whiff of mop water near
as we walk down the hall with cheer."

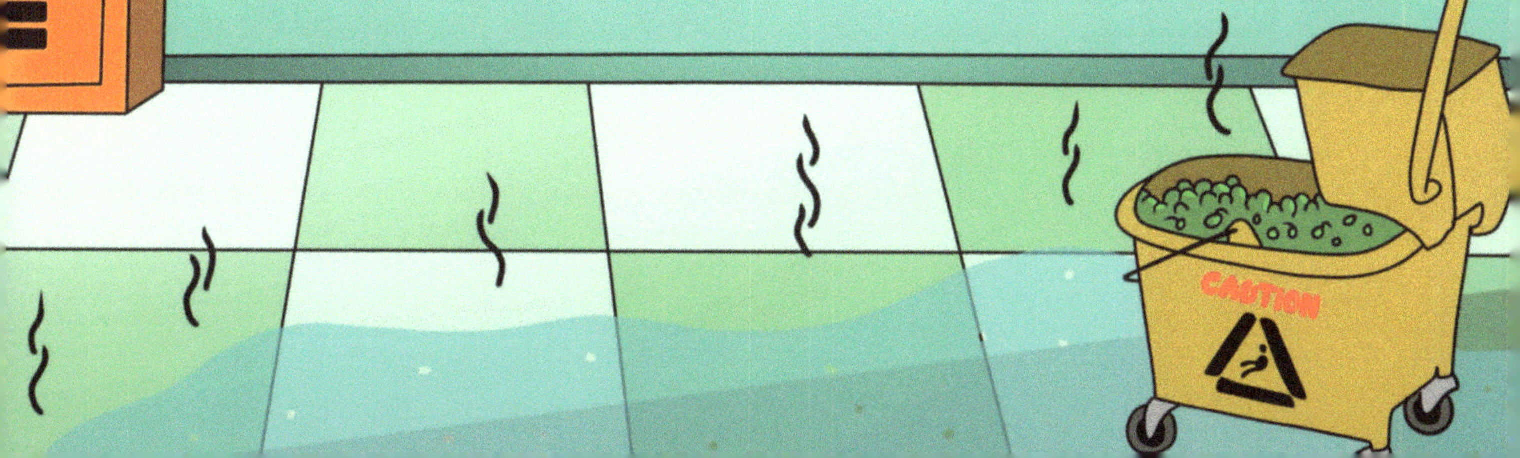

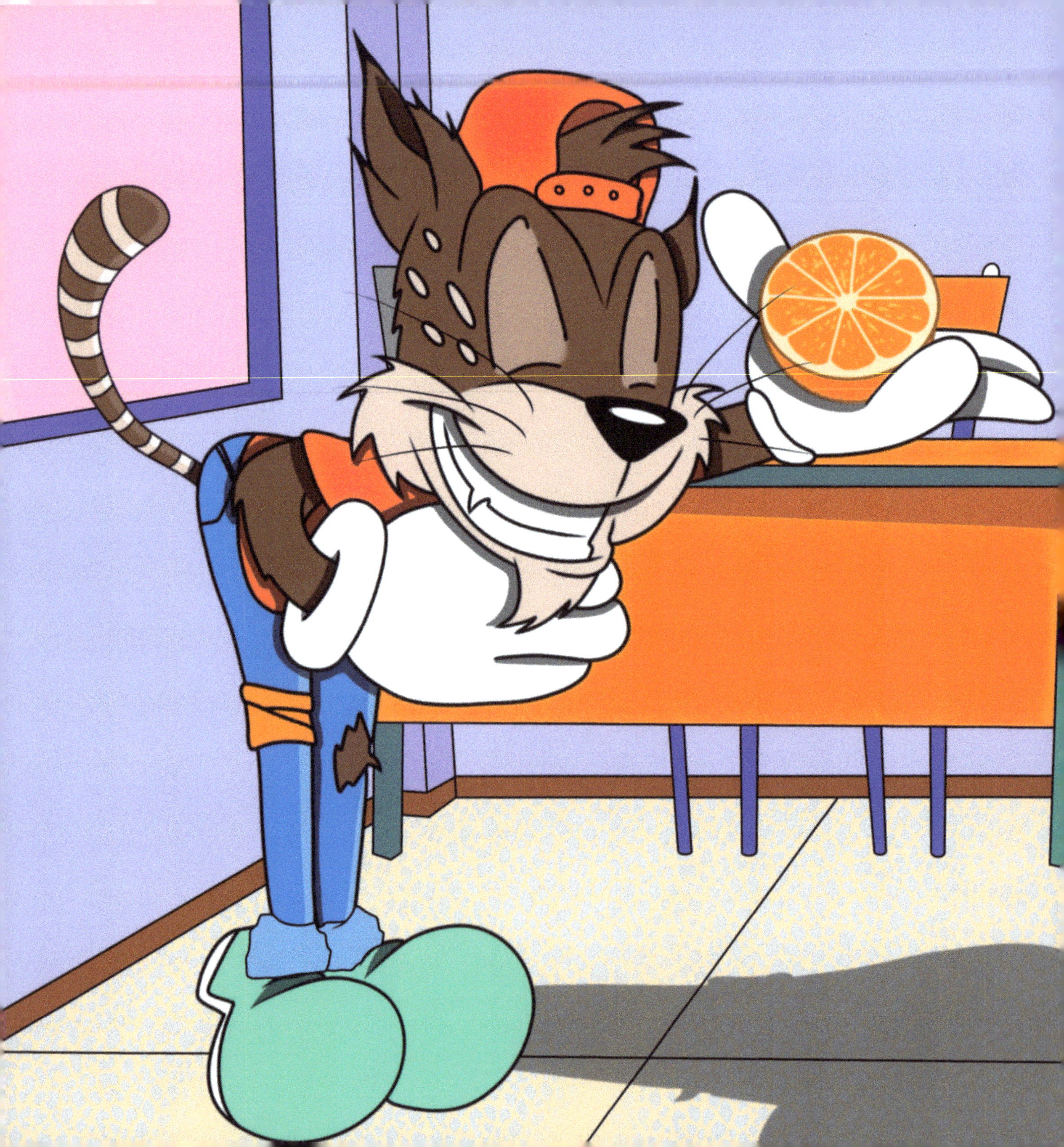

"So homies, listen up!
Now you're in the rhyming club.
I hope you use this skill at will
because now you know the drill.
Find new words that sound the same,
and by now you know my name.
It's Jack the Cat who does not upset,
nothing rhymes with orange, you bet!"

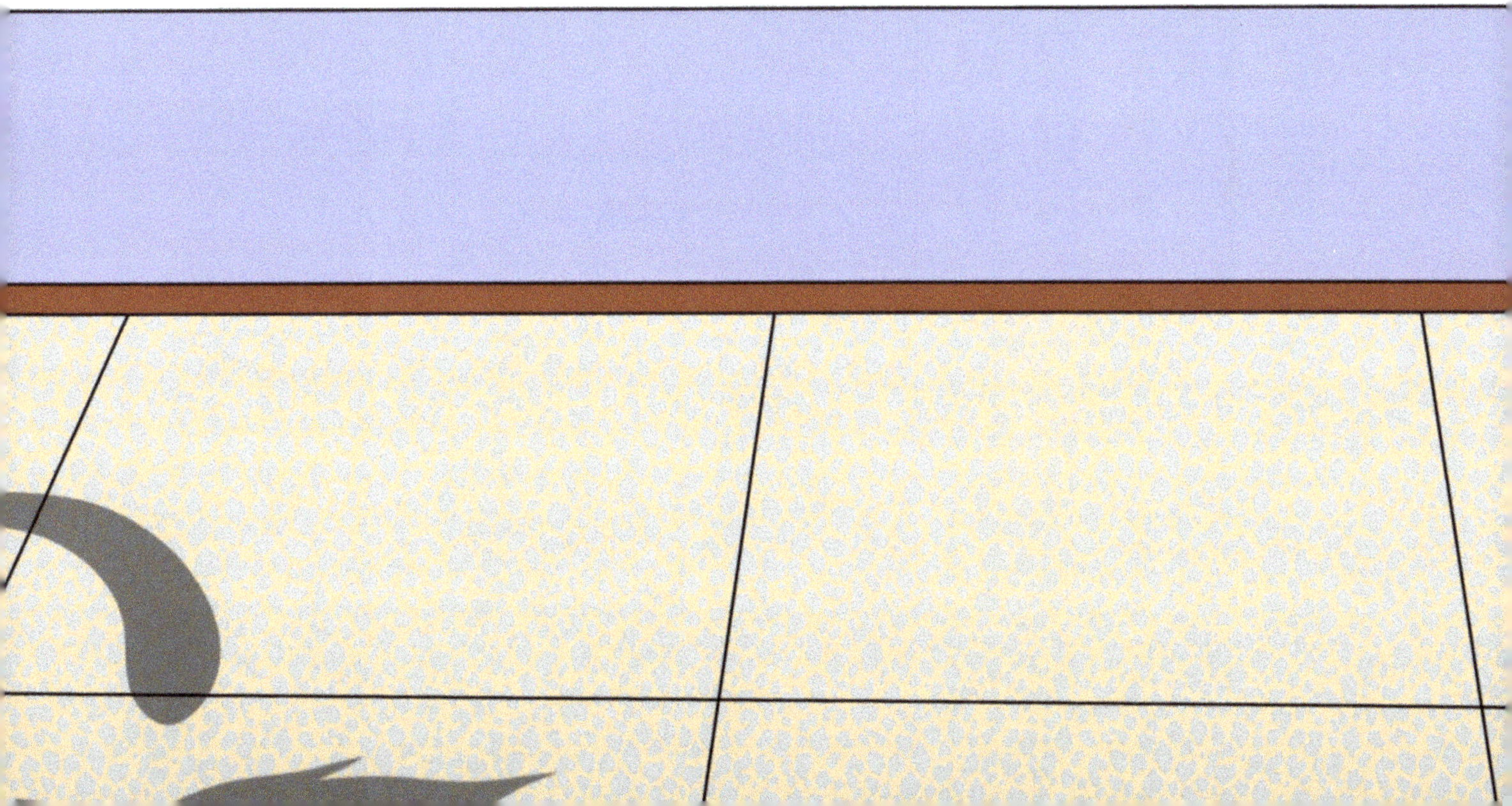

Glossary

"Breaking fast" – to eat food for the first time after fasting or not eating for a period of time.

Dedication – the quality of being dedicated or committed to a task or purpose.

Desire – strongly wish or want for something.

Mediocre – of only moderate quality; not very good.

Mingle – mix or cause to mix together.

Peculiar – strange or odd; unusual.

Phrase – A small group of words standing together as a conceptual unit, typically forming a component of a clause.

Precision – the quality, condition, or fact of being exact and accurate.

Prowl – (of a person or animal) move around restlessly and stealthily, especially in search of or as if in search of prey.

Rhyme – correspondence of sound between words or the endings of words, especially when these are used at the ends of lines of poetry.

Retire – withdraw to or from a particular place.

Unique – being the only one of its kind; unlike anything else.

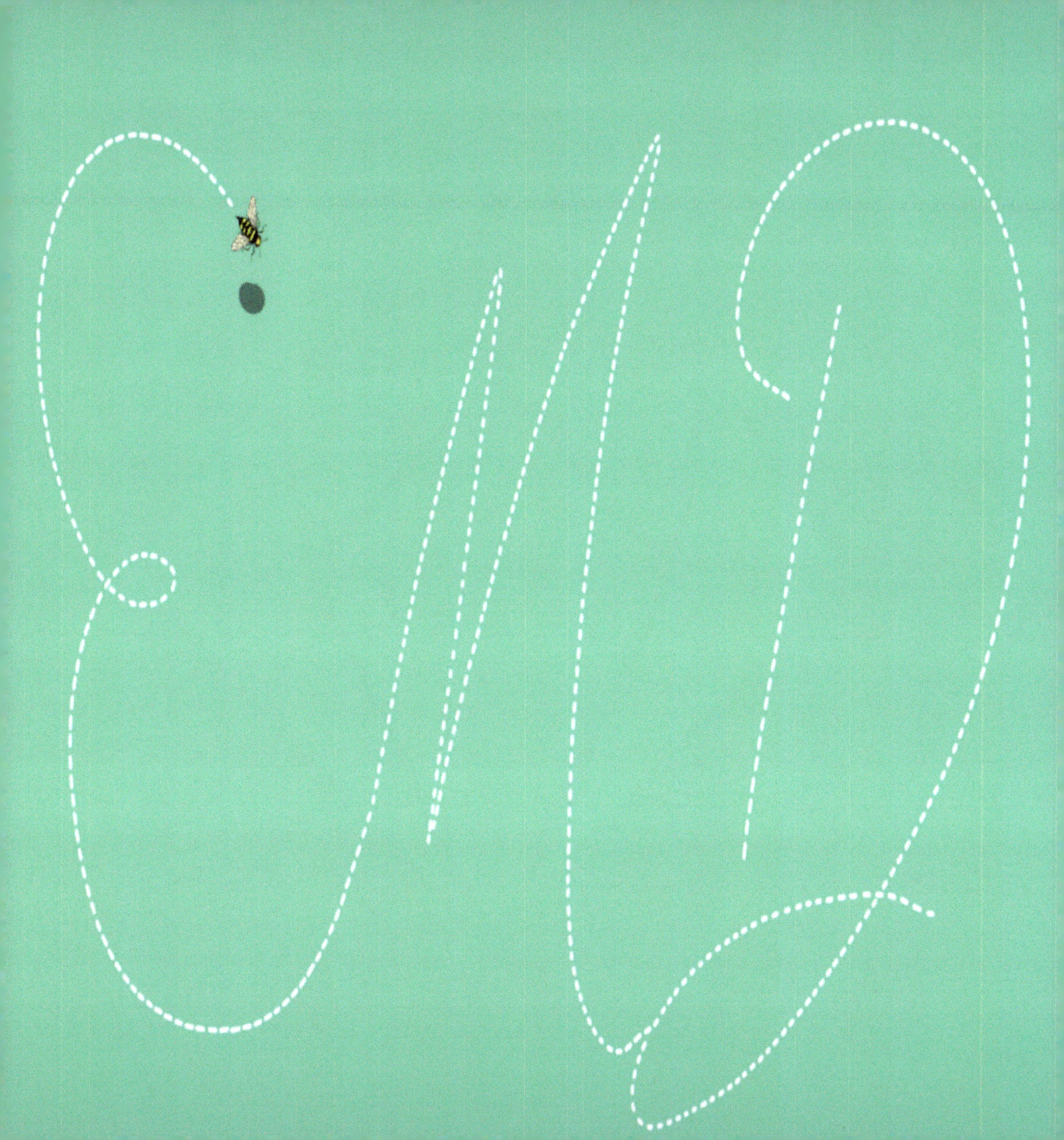

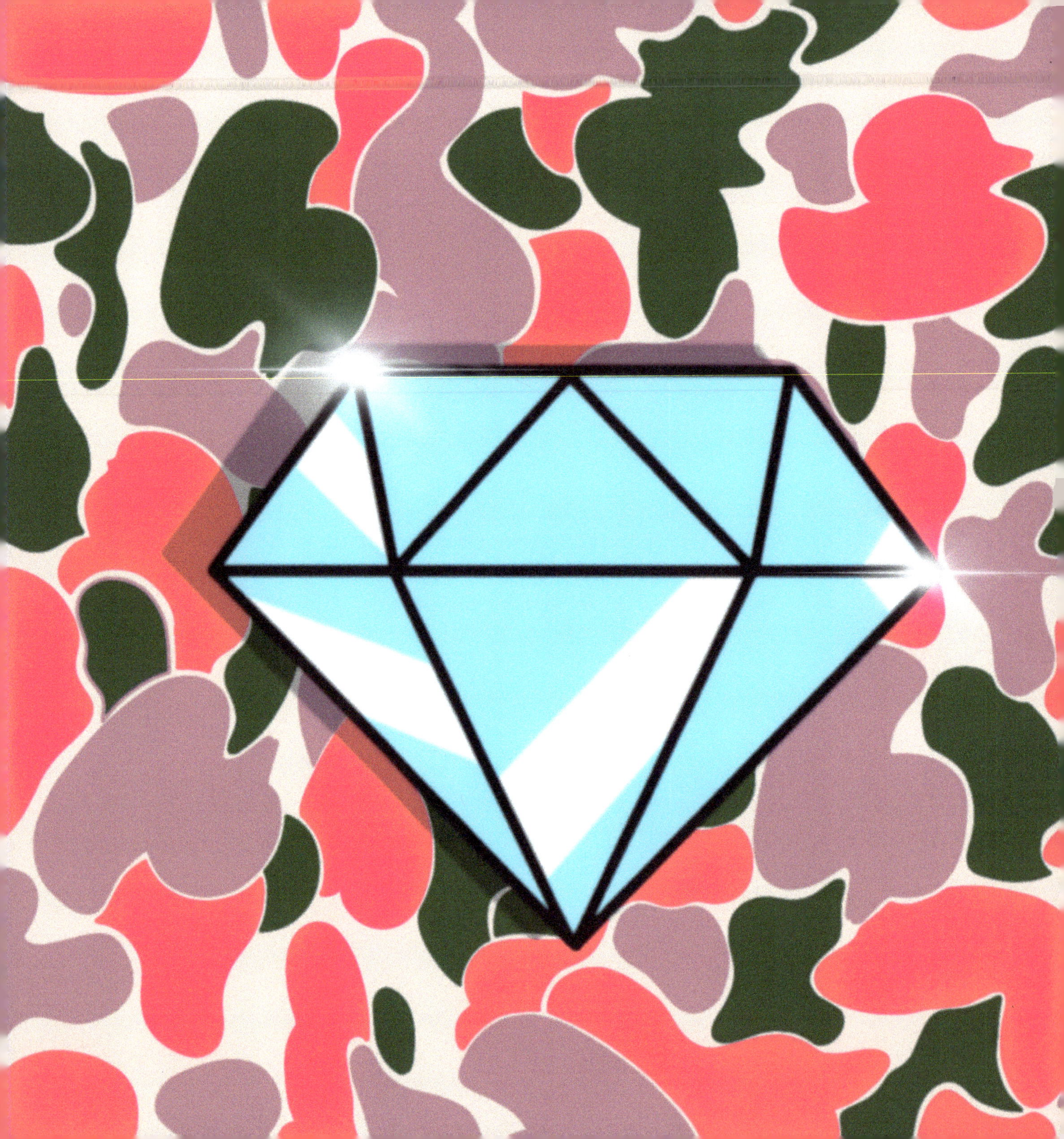

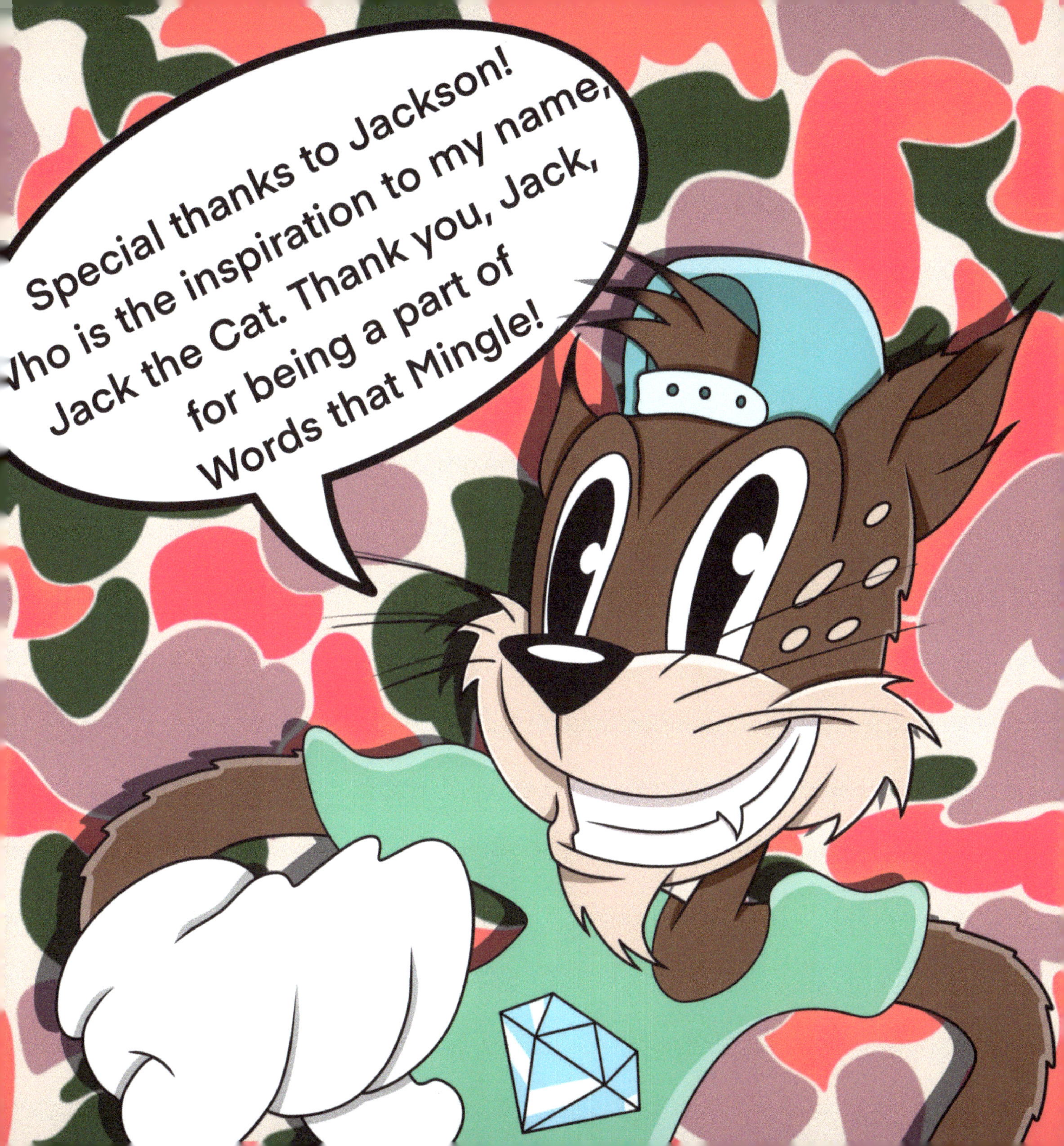
Special thanks to Jackson!
Who is the inspiration to my name,
Jack the Cat. Thank you, Jack,
for being a part of
Words that Mingle!

www.ingramcontent.com/pod-product-compliance
Ingram Content Group UK Ltd.
Pitfield, Milton Keynes, MK11 3LW, UK
UKHW060121010826
14089UKWH00006B/90

9 798218 214852